Reproducible Activities

Using the Standards
Building Grammar & Writing Skills

Grade 6

By
Cindy Barden

Published by Instructional Fair • TS Denison
an imprint of

Author: Cindy Barden
Editor: Jerry Aten

 **Children's Publishing**

Published by Instructional Fair • TS Denison
An imprint of McGraw-Hill Children's Publishing
Copyright © 2003 McGraw-Hill Children's Publishing

All Rights Reserved • Printed in the United States of America

Limited Reproduction Permission: Permission to duplicate these materials is limited to the person for whom they are purchased. Reproduction for an entire school or school district is unlawful and strictly prohibited.

Send all inquiries to:
McGraw-Hill Children's Publishing
3195 Wilson Drive NW
Grand Rapids, Michigan 49544

Using the Standards: Building Grammar & Writing Skills—grade 6
ISBN: 0-7424-1806-5

2 3 4 5 6 7 8 9 PHXBK 08 07 06 05 04 03

The *McGraw·Hill* Companies

Introduction

The vision guiding the (IRA) International Reading Association Standards and the (NCTE) National Council of Teachers of English is that all students must have the opportunities and resources to develop the language skills they need to pursue life's goals and to participate fully as informed, productive members of society.

The NCTE/IRA Standards are not prescriptions for particular curriculum or instruction; they are not distinct and separable; they are, in fact, interrelated and should be considered as a whole. The goal of the activities in this book is to provide the means for students to meet those standards by mastering the many skills needed for written communication.

The list of twelve standards is presented on the next page. The table of contents includes a column in which the number of each standard that applies to a particular activity is indicated. Teachers and parents can use this as an at-a-glance guide to the standard(s) addressed in each activity. In addition, the specific skill in focus for the activity is included in the upper right hand corner of that page.

English Language Arts Standards

1. Read a wide range of texts.

2. Read a wide range of literature.

3. Apply a variety of strategies to comprehend and interpret texts.

4. Use spoken, written, and visual language to communicate effectively.

5. Use a variety of strategies while writing and use elements of the writing process to communicate.

6. Apply knowledge of language structure and conventions, media techniques, figurative language, and genre to create, critique, and discuss texts.

7. Research issues and interests, pose questions, and gather data to communicate discoveries.

8. Work with a variety of technological and other resources to collect information and to communicate knowledge.

9. Understand and respect the differences in language use across cultures, regions, and social roles.

10. Students whose first language is not English use their first language to develop competencies in English and other content areas.

11. Participate in a variety of literary communities.

12. Use spoken, written, and visual language to accomplish purposes.

Activities	Standards Reflected	Page
Grammar		
Names and Titles	4, 6	9
Words in Titles	4, 6	10
Days, Months, Events, and Organizations	4, 6	11
Place Names	4, 6	12
More Words to Capitalize	4, 6	13
Capitalization Review	4, 6, 7	14
Periods, Question Marks, and Exclamation Marks	4, 6	15
Commas Separate	4, 6	16
More Ways to Use Commas	4, 6	17
Introducing: The Colon	4, 6	18
Use These Sparingly	4, 6	19
Titles	4, 6	20
"Use Quotation Marks," He Said	4, 6	21
Punctuation Review	4, 6	22
More Than One	4, 6	23
More Unusual Noun Plurals	4, 6	24
Apostrophes Show Possession	4, 6, 7, 9	25
Ready, Set, Action	4, 6	26
Present, Past, and Future	4, 5, 6	27
Verbs Link	4, 6	28
I Am, She Was, He Will Be	4, 6	29
Present, Past, and Past Participle	4, 6	30
Go, Went, Gone	4, 6	31
In Agreement	4, 6	32
She = Sue	4, 6	33
Yours and Mine	4, 6	34
She = Aunt, Lawyer, Mother	4, 6	35
Anybody Home?	4, 6	36
A Big, Red, Juicy Apple	4, 6, 9	37
Positive, Comparative, and Superlative Adjectives	4, 6	38
Hot, Hotter, Hottest	4, 6	39
Now or Later?	4, 6, 9	40
Positive, Comparative, and Superlative Adverbs	4, 6, 8	41
In, On, Under, and Through	4, 6	42
Aha!	4, 6	43

Table of Contents	Standards Reflected	Page
It's About Time	4, 6	44
One Plus One = One	4, 6	45
Parts of Speech Review	4, 6, 7	46
Writing		
From Beginning to End	4, 6, 7	47
Proofreading Symbols	4, 6, 7	48
Focus on a Topic	4, 6, 7	49
Compare and Contrast	4, 6, 12	50
Preparing an Outline	4, 6, 12	51
Writing Complete Sentences	4, 6	52
Stop and Take a Breath	4, 6	53
He Ran. She Ran.	4, 6	54
At the Beginning	4, 5, 6	55
In the Middle	4, 5, 6	56
At the End	4, 6, 7	57
Reasonable or Unreasonable?	4, 6, 7	58
Review	4, 5, 6, 7	59
Look Up, Down, and All Around	4, 6, 12	60
Laughed, Giggled, Chuckled, and Guffawed	4, 6, 8	61
Who Will Read It?	4, 6, 9, 12	62
Show, Don't Tell	4, 6, 8	63
More Interesting Words	4, 6, 8	64
To Entertain, Inform, and Persuade	4, 6, 12	65
You'll Never Believe What Happened!	4, 6, 12	66
Pizza Tastes Better Than Spinach	4, 6, 12	67
In My Opinion	4, 6, 12	68
Put a Can of Tuna in a Bowl	4, 6, 12	69
Don't Forget the Obvious	4, 6, 12	70
Don't Be Confused	4, 6, 8	71
Peanut Butter and Banana Sandwiches	4, 6, 12	72
Houseboats, Igloos, and Tents	4, 6, 12	73
For Your Information	4, 6, 8	74
Where Would You Find It?	4, 6, 8	75
Alike and Different	4, 6, 7	76
Blue or Green?	4, 6, 7	77
Because She Was Late	4, 6, 7	78
The Main Facts First	3, 4, 6, 7	79
Matching	4, 6, 7	80

Table of Contents	Standards Reflected	Page
What If Questions	4, 6, 7	81
What If Answers	4, 6, 7	82
And Then What Happened?	4, 6, 12	83
The Very First Time	4, 6, 12	84
Ask Questions	4, 6, 7	85
Gather Answers	4, 6, 7	86
Sweet, Sour, Bright, Slippery, Loud	4, 6	87
Water, Water, All Around	4, 6, 12	88
Describe Your Neighborhood	4, 6, 12	89
Characters, Settings, and Plots	4, 6, 12	90
Conclusions and Themes	4, 6, 12	91
Someone Has Been Eating My Porridge	4, 6	92
Review a Book	4, 6, 7	93
Bring Characters to Life	4, 6, 12	94
Personality Traits	4, 6, 12	95
What Did They Say?	4, 6, 9	96
When and Where?	4, 6, 12	97
Overcoming Obstacles	4, 6, 12	98
The Quest	4, 6, 12	99
Did They Live Happily Ever After?	4, 6, 12	100
Review and Write	4, 6, 7	101
Dear Friend,	4, 6, 12	102
Thank You for the Wonderful Service	4, 6, 12	103
Who? What? When? Where? Why? How?	1, 4, 6, 12	104
From More Important to Less Important	1, 4, 6, 12	105
Short and to the Point	4, 6, 12	106
You're in the News	4, 6, 12	107
The Fall from the Wall	4, 6, 12	108
Book Reports with a Twist	2, 4, 6, 8, 12	109
A History of the World from Then Until Now	4, 6, 8, 12	110
Begin Your Research	4, 6, 8	111
Organize Before You Write	4, 6, 7, 12	112
True or False?	4, 6, 7	113
Leap Tall Buildings	4, 6, 12	114
Super Character Saves Earth	4, 6, 12	115
To the Rescue	4, 6	116
Poetry	4, 6, 9	117
The Moon in June	4, 6, 9	118

Table of Contents	Standards Reflected	Page
Give a Hoot: Don't Pollute	4, 6, 9, 12	119
Winter	4, 6, 9, 12	120
The Cloud Is a Pillow	4, 6, 12	121
Acrostics	4, 6, 8, 12	122
Repetition	4, 6, 9, 12	123
Revising and Editing Checklist		124
Answer Key		125

Capitalization: Proper Nouns

Name _____ Date _____

Names and Titles

Capitalize people's names.
    Mary Todd Lincoln   Gertrude Stein
    Horace Mann

Capitalize people's initials.
    John F. Kennedy   F. Scott Fitzgerald
    J.R.R. Tolkien

Capitalize a person's title when used with his or her name.
    Captain Kirk   President Wilson
    Sergeant Preston   King Henry

Capitalize abbreviations of titles when used with people's names.
    Mr. Spock   Dr. Watson
    Col. Burns   Ms. Frizzle

Do not capitalize titles if they do not refer to a specific person.
    Josh ran for mayor.
    Sara was promoted to lieutenant.
    Sandy studied to be a doctor.

Capitalize animals' names.
    Shamu   Lassie
    Fido   Spot

Circle all words that should be capitalized.
1. jonah walton had been a doctor for many years before he ran for Congress.
2. Some people did not know if they should address him as dr. walton or senator walton.
3. Did you meet colonel sylvia s. smith when she ran for mayor?
4. I think mayor smith has done a great job so far.
5. At Ocean World, we swam with a dolphin named footsie and fed grumpy, the whale.

Capitalization

Name _____ Date _____

Words in Titles

Capitalize the first word and last word in titles of books, poems, movies, magazines, works of art, songs, important documents, and newspapers.
    Magna Carta   Tom Sawyer
    The New York Times

Capitalize all nouns, verbs, adjectives, and adverbs in titles.
    "The Three Little Pigs"   Lassie Come Home

Do not capitalize: *a, an, the, and, or, nor,* or *but* unless they are the first or last words in the title.
    George and Martha   Angus and the Ducks

Do not capitalize short prepositions unless they are the first or last words in a title. (Short prepositions are ones with four or fewer letters, such as *of, to, in,* and *out*.)
    The Wizard of Oz   Gone with the Wind
    The Last of the Mohicans   Declaration of Independence
    Harry Potter and the Sorcerer's Stone

1. List the titles of four books or stories.
    Harry Potter and the order of Pheneox   Holes
    The Push cart War   Amelies note book

2. List the titles of four movies.
    Holes   Freinds
    The Haunted machion   Snow White

3. List the names of four songs.
    London Brige is falling down   Hot cross buns
    Twinkle Twinkle little stars   Jingle bells

4. What newspapers and magazines do members of your family read?
    The columbus dispach   ?
    ?   ?

Name _____ Date _____

Capitalization

Days, Months, Events, and Organizations

Capitalize the names of months of the year and days of the week.
    January   Saturday
    March

Capitalize the names of holidays.
    Easter   Kwanza
    Hanukkah

Capitalize the names of specific historical events.
    World War II   Industrial Revolution
    Roaring Twenties

Capitalize the names of specific events.
    the World Series   Super Bowl
    the Olympics

Capitalize the names of specific organizations.
    Girl Scouts   National Football League
    Elks Club

Capitalize specific brand names and names of companies.
    General Electric   Mustang
    Kleenex

Underline all words that should be capitalized.
1. Many types of cars, like the <u>pacer</u>, <u>edsel</u>, and <u>gremlin</u> are no longer made.
2. If you could attend a major sporting event, would you rather go to the <u>super bowl</u>, the <u>stanley cup playoffs</u>, or the <u>kentucky derby</u>?
3. <u>josh</u> belongs to the <u>boy scouts</u>, pitches in little league, and was elected president of the <u>lakeside stamp club</u> last <u>march</u>.
4. <u>independence day</u>, <u>presidents day</u>, <u>memorial day</u>, <u>labor day</u>, and <u>christmas</u> are all legal holidays.
5. The students were given a choice of writing about the <u>revolutionary war</u>, the <u>reconstruction era</u>, the <u>industrial revolution</u>, or the <u>civil war</u> as topics for their history reports.

Name _____ Date _____

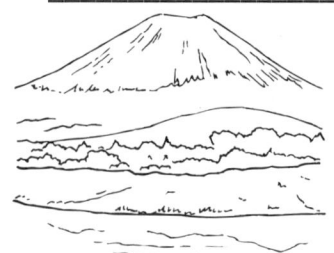

Place Names

Capitalization

Capitalize the names of specific places.
Write a second example for each type of place.

Place Type	Example	Your Example
Cities	Paris	columbus
Counties	Washara	fairfax
States	Louisiana	Ohio
Countries	Sri Lanka	Taiwan
Lakes	Lake Michigan	日月 tan lake
Rivers	Amazon River	ohio river
Oceans	Indian Ocean	Pacific ocean
Seas	Red Sea	seashore (somkin)
Mountains	Mount McKinley	Mount Blanc
Mountain Ranges	Rocky Mountains	Appalatian mt
Volcanoes	Mount St. Helens	Mount Fugi
Parks	Yellowstone National Park	regular park
Planets	Pluto	earth
Galaxies	Andromeda	milky way
Streets	First Avenue	Westcase
Historical Sites	Tomb of the Unknown Soldier	
Schools	Franklin Elementary	Wright Elementary
Colleges	Harvard University	ohio state University
Theaters	Retlaw Theater	Dollar Theater
Religious Buildings	Mormon Tabernacle	Church
Museums	Museum of Fine Art	some kind of museum

More Words to Capitalize

Capitalize the pronoun *I*.

Capitalize the first word of every sentence.
    The quick brown fox jumped over the lazy dog.
    Once upon a time, a poor woodcutter lived in a forest.

Capitalize the first word of each line in most poetry.
    Hickory, dickory dock,
    The mouse ran up the clock.
    The clock struck one,
    And down he run . . .

Capitalize the first word in the greeting of a letter.
    Greetings,   Dear Mr. Bunyan:

Capitalize all other nouns in the greeting of a letter.
    Dear Major: Dear Sir:

Capitalize the first word in the closing of a letter.
    Yours truly,   Sincerely yours,

Underline the words that should be capitalized.
1. dear king:
2. i am planning to visit your famous wall on the first of may.
3. will that date be acceptable to you?
4. yours truly,
5. humpty dumpty, professor
6. dear professor dumpty:
7. queen anne and i look forward to your visit.
8. will you be doing any of your famous wall-sitting stunts that day?
9. i'll assign my best horses and men to protect you.
10. the queen has asked her friend, mother goose, to write special a poem about your visit in may.
11. sincerely yours,
12. king leo

Name _____ Date _____

Capitalization Review

Complete the sentences. Use correct capitalization.

1. The last movie I watched was __I Dont know__.
2. Some of my ancestors lived in __Taiwain__.
3. I was born on a __Thursday__ in __June__.
   (day of the week)   (name of month)
4. My favorite holiday is __Christmas.__
5. The person I admire most is __me__.
6. My favorite story when I was little was "__Yada Yada__."
7. One of my favorite authors is __Roald Dahl__.
8. __Europe__ is a great place to visit.
9. We went to __Japan__ on our vacation.
10. The boat sailed across __an ocean__.

Circle A or B to show which group of words is capitalized correctly.

11. A. Egyptian pyramids   (B.) Egyptian Pyramids
12. A. a Jewish holiday   (B.) a Jewish Holiday
13. A. italian spaghetti   (B.) Italian spaghetti
14. (A.) *A Tale of Two Cities*   B. *A Tale of two Cities*
15. A. Mexico city, Mexico   (B.) Mexico City, Mexico
16. (A.) Sincerely yours,   B. Sincerely Yours,
17. A. "Androcles and the lion" (B.) "Androcles and the Lion"

End Punctuation

Name _____ Date _____

Periods, Question Marks, and Exclamation Marks

All sentences need end punctuation.

A declarative sentence makes a statement. It ends with a period.
    Hawaii became a state in 1965.

An imperative sentence tells someone to do something. It also ends with a period.
    See the volcanoes if you go to Hawaii.

A period is also used after initials and abbreviations.
    P.T. Barnum   Tues.

An exclamatory sentence shows surprise. Use an exclamation mark at the end.
    We won!

An interrogative sentence asks a question and ends with a question mark.
    What time does the plane leave?

Write *declarative, imperative, exclamatory,* or *interrogative* before each sentence. Add end punctuation. Add periods after initials and abbreviations.

1. _____ Where are you going on your next vacation
2. _____ Grandmother asked me to help her on Tuesday
3. _____ Don't slam the door when you leave
4. _____ Always be on time
5. _____ Will you be on time
6. _____ It is important to be on time
7. _____ Hurry, we're late
8. _____ Sgt Burns, go to the colonel's office
9. _____ Dr J C Brown taught at Harvard
10. _____ U S Grant was a popular president

Commas

Name _____ Date _____

Commas Separate

Use a comma after the greeting in a friendly letter.
    Dear Mary,   Greetings,

Use a comma after the closing in a letter.
    Yours truly,   Sincerely,

"I need a comma so I can pause."

Use commas to separate three or more items in a series. Use a comma after each word or phrase in the series except the last one.
    He planted cabbages, beans, turnips, and broccoli in the garden.
    She mowed the lawn, trimmed the bushes, and raked the yard.
    Cassie, Jake, Rachel, and Tobias went to the beach.
    The waves washed away their large, elegant and stately sand castle.

Use a comma to separate an ordinal number from the rest of the sentence if it is not used as an adjective.
    First, you should open the window.
    Second, add the anchovies.
    He won second place in the contest. [no comma]
    Who came in tenth? [no comma]

Use a comma to separate the name of a city and state or city and country.
    Portland, Maine   Seoul, South Korea

Add commas and end punctuation.

1. The big red fragrant rose won first prize at the flower show
2. Dear Aunt June
3. Will you bring chips soda plates and napkins for the picnic
4. Third place the chairs tables and benches along the east wall
5. Can you stop at the store go to the post office and take the garbage out today
6. How was your trip to Moscow Russia

More Ways to Use Commas

Use a comma to separate an introductory word or group of words from the rest of the sentence.
    Although he tried his best, Marcus came in last.
    Unfortunately, he missed the haystack.

Use commas to set off words of direct address.
    Come here, Suzanne.
    Tomas C. Rodriquez, watch out for that rock!
    Look, Max, it's a hummingbird.

Use commas to separate months and days from years.
    September 11, 2001   October 12, 1492

Use commas to separate days of the week from dates.
    Saturday, January 10, 1904   Friday, October 13

Do not use commas to separate months and years if the date is not included.
    July 1776   March 1967

1. Write your birth date. _____
2. When did you begin first grade? _____
                             (month and year)
3. What city and state do you live in? _____
4. What is today's day, date, and year? _____

Add commas where needed.

5. "Listen my children and you shall hear of the midnight ride of Paul Revere." ("Paul Revere's Ride" by Henry W. Longfellow)
6. Although Longfellow made Paul Revere a hero in the poem Revere was arrested by British soldiers and never completed his famous ride.
7. Because they confiscated his horse Paul Revere never arrived at Concord Massachusetts before the battle on April 19 1775.
8. Samuel Prescott the man who warned the rebels about the approach of the British Army isn't even mentioned in the famous poem.

Introducing: The Colon

Use a colon to separate hours and minutes.
    10:15   2:47

Use a colon to introduce a list of items.
    When you get to the store, please pick up three things: bread, milk, and eggs.
    We need the following items for the party: soda, chips, hot dogs, buns, pickles, onions, catsup, relish, and mustard.

Use a colon after the greeting in a business letter.
    Dear Madam: Dear Product Director:
    Dear Professor White:

Use a colon to introduce and emphasize a word, phrase, or quotation.
    Janice has only one thing on her mind: attending the party.
    During the camping trip, he had two kinds of luck: bad and none.
    Above all, remember this: Every cloud has a silver lining.

Do not use a colon immediately after a verb.
    I like pizza, spaghetti, lasagna, and tacos.
    She can play the banjo, tap dance, and whistle at the same time.

Write *Yes* or *No* to indicate whether the colons are used correctly.

1. ____ Will you be ready by 9:15?
2. ____ He forgot one important step: to defrost the chicken first.
3. ____ Dear Mother:
4. ____ Will you help: rake the lawn, take out the trash, and wash the dog?
5. ____ The movie begins at: 2:07.
6. ____ The hats came in three colors red: white: or blue.

Semicolons and Dashes

Name _____ Date _____

Use These Sparingly

Semicolons indicate a bit more of a pause than a comma, but not as much as a period. They should be used sparingly.

Use a semicolon to connect independent clauses not joined by *and, but, or, nor, for,* or *yet.* An independent clause is a group of words that could be a complete sentence.
    Mary forgot; Jason remembered; Ebony didn't care.
    Isaac is an excellent musician; he makes few mistakes.

Write an independent clause after the semicolon to complete the sentence.

1. Home is where you hang your hat; _____
_____

Use semicolons with words or phrases in a series instead of commas in cases where commas are needed for other reasons.
    His business trip took him to Tokyo, Japan; London, England; and Moscow, Russia.
    Would you like to see the doctor on Monday, September 16; Wednesday, September 24; or Friday, September 27?

A dash is usually written as two hyphens side by side with no space between the dash and the words on either side of it. On the computer it is a special character known as an "em dash."

A dash is used to connect groups of words to other groups.
    The secret to becoming wealthy is this--make more than you spend--and do it for a long time.
    Linda--the one who never bothered to visit--inherited only her mother's dust collection.

A dash can be used to attach material to the end of a sentence when there is a break in the flow.
    The president probably will be reelected--unless something drastic happens soon.
    I doubt if you will find a gold mine or an oil well in your backyard--but miracles can happen.

2. Write a sentence using a dash correctly.
_____
_____

Name _____ Date _____

Titles

Use quotation marks around the titles of
    Songs: "Twinkle, Twinkle, Little Star"
    Poems: "Little Bo Peep"
    Book Chapters: "Anne's Confessions"
    Short stories: "Cinderella"
    Magazine articles: "50 Ways to Get Straight A's"

The names of books, plays, movies, television series, works of art, magazines, and newspapers should be underlined or typed in italics, not in quotation marks.
    <u>Charlotte's Web</u>   The *New York Times*

Use quotation marks to enclose all words quoted from a source.
    "Four score and seven years ago…"
    "When in the course of human events…"

Note that the ellipsis (…) indicates that the sentence quoted continues, but those words are not included.

On the blanks, write *A* if the words should be in quotation marks or *B* if the title should be underlined/italicized.

1. _____ The Lord of the Rings (a movie)
2. _____ Mary Had a Little Lamb (a song)
3. _____ Superfudge (a book)
4. _____ Newsweek (a magazine)
5. _____ Hey, Diddle, Diddle (poem)

Enclose the exact words of a speaker in quotation marks.
Patrick Henry said, "Give me liberty or give me death."

If the exact words of the speaker are not used, no quotation marks are needed.
    Patrick Henry said he didn't want to live if he couldn't be free.

Write *direct* or *indirect* on the blanks. If the words are a direct quote, add quotation marks.

6. _____ The child cried, I want to go home now.
7. _____ The child cried because he wanted to go home.

Name _____   Date _____

"Use Quotation Marks," He Said

In addition to using quotation marks correctly, writers need to know when to capitalize words and where to put quotation marks, commas, periods, question marks, and exclamation marks.

A direct quotation begins with a capital letter.
　　The coach shouted, "That was a great play!"

When a quoted sentence is interrupted by words that are not part of the quotation, the second part of the sentence does not begin with a capital letter, and a comma is used to set apart words not said by the speaker.
　　"That," said the coach, "was a great play."

If a quotation includes end punctuation, it is not necessary to add a comma between the quoted words and the rest of the sentence.
　　"That was a great play!" shouted the coach.

When a quotation comes at the end of a sentence, enclose end punctuation inside the quotation marks.
　　He said, "Let's head for home."
　　She asked, "Why did you bring your dog?"

When a quotation is an interrogatory sentence, use a question mark instead of a comma.
　　"Will you be there by 10:15?" asked Todd.

When a quotation is an exclamatory sentence, use an exclamation mark instead of a comma.
　　"Look out!" shouted Bessie.

Add quotation marks, commas, and end punctuation to the following sentences.

1. Today said Mr. Cunningham we are going on a field trip
2. Where are we going asked Marie
3. I know shouted Bert We're going to the candle factory
4. No replied Mr. Cunningham our plans have changed
5. Maybe we could go to the cookie factory suggested Tasha
6. It's a surprise said Mr. Cunningham You'll find out when we get there

Name _____ Date _____

Punctuation Review

1. Include a quotation in a declarative sentence about your hometown.
_____
_____

2. Use a colon in an imperative sentence about wearing seat belts.
_____
_____

3. Write an exclamatory sentence about a possible danger.
_____
_____

4. Include three or more items in a series in an interrogative sentence about a party.
_____
_____

5. Write a sentence using an abbreviation, date, and time.
_____
_____
_____

Add semicolons to this sentence.

6. Important dates in American history include April 19, 1775 July 4, 1776 October 19, 1781 and September 1, 1783.

Fill in the blanks.

7. Use _____ to enclose the exact words of a speaker.
8. Use a _____ at the end of an interrogative sentence.
9. Use a _____ after an initial or abbreviation.
10. Use a _____ to introduce a list of items.
11. Use a _____ to separate a series of items.
12. Use a _____ after the greeting in a business letter.
13. Use a _____ to separate the name of a city and state.
14. Use a _____ to connect independent clauses.

Singular and Plural Nouns

Name _____ Date _____

More Than One

Nouns are names of persons, places, things, or ideas. *Child, park, shoe, cat,* and **freedom** are nouns.

Nouns can be singular or plural. Singular means one. Plural means more than one. To change a singular noun to plural, add an *s* to most nouns.

There are many exceptions, however.

If a noun ends in -ch, -sh, -x, -z, or -s, add -es to form the plural.
    Examples: pass passes   arch arches
                         marsh marshes   glass glasses

Write the plurals for these nouns.

1. march _____
2. sketch _____
3. ash _____
4. radish _____
5. wrench _____
6. watch _____
7. box _____
8. church _____
9. peach _____
10. fox _____
11. wish _____
12. dish _____
13. match _____
14. bush _____

To form the plural of most nouns that end in y, change the y to an i and add es. When in doubt, check a dictionary.
    Exceptions: If the final -y is preceded by a vowel, add -s.
    Examples: sky skies   fly flies
                          jay jays   joy joys

Write the plurals for these nouns.

15. boy _____
16. jelly _____
17. berry _____
18. galaxy _____
19. day _____
20. nanny _____
21. display _____
22. pay _____
23. agency _____
24. toy _____
25. family _____
26. baby _____
27. tray _____
28. penny _____
29. way _____
30. melody _____

Name _____   Date _____

More Unusual Noun Plurals

To form the plural of many nouns that end in -f or -fe, change the -f or -fe to a -v and add -es. There are so many exceptions to this rule, however, that it is best to check a dictionary if you aren't certain.

Examples: loaf loaves   knife knives
staff staffs   giraffe giraffes

1. self _____
2. wife _____
3. oaf _____
4. wolf _____
5. chef _____
6. roof _____
7. half _____
8. reef _____
9. thief _____
10. elf _____
11. leaf _____
12. life _____
13. calf _____
14. wharf _____
15. gulf _____
16. bluff _____
17. sheriff _____
18. chief _____

The spelling of some nouns remains the same for both the singular and the plural.
   Examples: deer, sheep, Sioux

The spelling of some nouns changes completely.
   Examples: child children   person people

Write the plural for these nouns. Use a dictionary if you need help.

19. man _____
20. woman _____
21. mouse _____
22. ox _____
23. foot _____
24. tooth _____

Possessive Nouns

Name _____ Date _____

Apostrophes Show Possession

Possessive nouns show ownership. To make a singular noun possessive, add an apostrophe and an -s.
   Example: president's campaign

If a plural noun already ends with -s, add only an apostrophe to show possession.
   Example: monkeys' tails

If a plural noun doesn't end in -s, add an apostrophe and -s.
   Example: women's rights

Write the correct form of the word given for each sentence in the set. Words may be singular, plural, singular possessive, or plural possessive.

student
   1. How many _____ are in your school?
   2. Where is that _____ book?
   3. All the _____ classes begin at 8:00.
   4. Which _____ is best at math?

writer
   5. Many _____ use computers.
   6. That _____ computer is an antique.
   7. That _____ made the best-seller list three times.
   8. They met at the _____ convention.

child
   9. All of the _____ went on the field trip.
   10. The _____ bus is ready to leave.
   11. That _____ nearly missed the bus.
   12. The _____ teacher gave him a wink.

mouse
   13. Seven _____ danced in the moonlight.
   14. One _____ was white.
   15. The white _____ tail was not very long.
   16. The other six _____ whiskers were short.

Active Verbs

Name _____ Date _____

Ready, Set, Action

Active verbs are words that express mental or physical action. *Run, shiver, pass,* and *shine* are active verbs.

Examples: She *studied* for the test.
He *jogged* through the park.

Every sentence must contain at least one verb to be a complete sentence. Many sentences contain more than one verb.

Underline the active verbs in each sentence.

1. Maria raked the leaves.
2. Tony thought of a new invention.
3. Tasha washed the dishes and put them away.
4. They cleaned, dusted, and polished the furniture.
5. While Josh worked, his little sister read a book.
6. Do you like ice cream?

Write active verbs in the blanks to complete the sentences.

7. Wanda _____ the floor before she _____ it.
8. At the park, Marta _____, _____, and _____.
9. Will you _____?
10. The parrot _____ to me.
11. Who _____ that tree?
12. Can you _____ with me?
13. Terri _____ to Australia.
14. Chad _____ his house.
15. After school, Miguel _____ to the park.

26

© McGraw-Hill Children's Publishing

0-7424-1806-5 Building Grammar & Writing Skills

Verb Tenses

Name _____ Date _____

Present, Past, and Future

Verb tense is used to express time. To explain what is happening right now, use the present tense.
   Example: He *is dancing* well. He dances well.

To explain what has already happened, use the past tense. Add *-d* or *-ed* to form the past tense of most verbs.
   Example: *He danced* well last night at the party.

To explain what will happen, use the future tense.
   Example: He *will dance* well tomorrow in the contest.

Rewrite the sentences so all verbs in the sentence are in the same tense.

1. He walked, he is running, and then he skips._____
_____
2. She feels sad, but was not sure why._____
_____
3. They are my friends, and so was she._____
_____
4. He laughs and then he told us what was so funny._____
_____

Write sentences using the present tense of each verb.

5. walk_____
_____
6. rest_____
_____

Write sentences using the past tense of each verb.

7. paint_____
_____
8. hike_____
_____

Write a sentence using the future tense of each verb.

9. bake_____
_____
10. write_____
_____

Linking Verbs

Name _____ Date _____

Verbs Link

Linking verbs do not express mental or physical action. Linking verbs connect (or link) the subject with another word in the sentence.

Be is the most common linking verb. Forms of *be* include

am	is	are	was
were	has been	had been	have been
shall be	may be	can be	should be
would have been			

Other verbs commonly used as linking verbs are

taste	feel	smell	look
sound	appear	become	seem
grow	remain	stay	

Linking verbs can be used in all three tenses: present, past, and future.

Examples: (Present)   The train *is* fast.
(Past)   Marc Chagall *was* an artist.
(Future)   Mary White *will be* happy soon.

Circle the linking verbs. Underline the words linked by the verb.

1. Paris is the capital of France.
2. Nicole was bored with the movie.
3. Who will be the next president?
4. Sunday is the first day of spring.
5. Do you think we are lost?
6. Brrr! The water is too cold.
7. When she arrived, she was ten minutes late.
8. Apple pie is my favorite dessert.
9. The apple tasted fresh and crisp.
10. Kristie will be a good pianist some day.
11. That seems easy.
12. Something smells delicious!

Helping Verbs

Name _____ Date _____

I Am, She Was, He Will Be

Helping verbs help the main verb express action or make a statement.

Commonly used helping verbs are

am	is	are	was	were	be
been	has	have	had	do	does
did	may	might	must	can	could
shall	should	will	would		

Helping verbs can be used in present, past, and future tenses.
Examples: (Present) Keith *is eating* now.
(Past) Keith *was eating* breakfast.
(Future) Keith *will eat* in an hour.

Underline the helping verbs.

1. Brianna is helping me paint the cabin.
2. We are working together on it.
3. Her brother was painting this morning.
4. He will paint again later today.
5. Tomorrow we will paint the inside of the cabin.
6. We might run out of paint.
7. If we do, we can get more.

Rewrite the underlined verbs using helping verbs. The first is done as an example.

8. Tom says he plans to help paint.   is planning
9. He said he started to think about the job.   _____
10. Brianna and I think he stalls too long.   _____
11. Perhaps he hopes we will forget.   _____
12. Brianna and I remind him often.   _____

Principal Parts of Verbs

Name _____ Date _____

Present, Past, and Past Participle

Verbs have three principal parts: present, past, and past participle.

Regular verbs form the past tense by adding -d or -ed to the present tense.

The past participle is formed by using the past tense of a verb with a helping verb: have, has or had.

Examples: Present   Past   Past Participle
I *walk*.   I *walked*.   I *have* (or *had*) *walked*.
She *paints*.   She *painted*. He *has* (or *had*) *painted*.

Fill in the missing form of each verb. If you are unsure of the spelling, check a dictionary.

	Present	**Past**	**Past Participle**
1.	look	_____	have/has/had looked
2.	_____	planned	_____
3.	_____	_____	have/has/had closed
4.	wash	_____	_____
5.	_____	prepared	_____
6.	_____	_____	have/has/had joined
7.	invite	_____	_____
8.	_____	reached	_____
9.	approve	_____	_____
10.	_____	watched	_____
11.	create	_____	_____
12.	_____	_____	have/has/had biked
13.	_____	pulled	_____
14.	travel	_____	_____
15.	_____	scrubbed	_____
16.	dance	_____	_____

Irregular Verbs

Name _____ Date _____

Go, Went, Gone

The past tense of most verbs is formed by adding -ed. Verbs that do not follow this format are called irregular verbs. Irregular verbs change completely in the past and past participle forms.

The chart shows some irregular verbs.

Present	Past	Past Participle
go	went	have/has/had gone
do	did	have/has/had done
fly	flew	have/has/had flown
grow	grew	have/has/had grown
ride	rode	have/has/had ridden
see	saw	have/has/had seen
sing	sang	have/has/had sung
throw	threw	have/has/had thrown
begin	began	have/has/had begun
speak	spoke	have/has/had spoken
drink	drank	have/has/had drunk
know	knew	have/has/had known
eat	ate	have/has/had eaten
wear	wore	have/has/had worn

Examples: They *go* to school.
They *went* to school yesterday.
They *have gone* (or *had gone*) to school for many years.

Rewrite each sentence twice using the past tense (*a*) and the past participle (*b*) of the verb.

1. Todd begins swimming class today.
   a._____
   b._____

2. She wears shorts when it is hot.
   a._____
   b._____

3. Jamal drinks milk with breakfast.
   a._____
   b._____

4. Who is speaking to us?
   a._____
   b._____

Agreement of Subjects and Predicates

Name _____ Date _____

In Agreement

The subject tells who or what a sentence is about. The subject of a sentence is always a noun or pronoun. Sentences can have more than one subject.
   Example: *Tomas* and *I* went to the mall.

The predicate tells what the subject does, did, is doing, or will do. Predicates can be more than one word. A sentence can have more than one predicate.
   Example: She *walked* to the store but then *ran* home.

All complete sentences must have a subject and a predicate.

If the subject of a sentence is singular, the verb in the predicate must be singular. If the subject is plural, the verb must be plural.

   Examples: The *cat* with the black stripes *is* napping.
   The *cats* in the yard *are* awake.

Write the singular or plural form of the subject in each sentence to match the verb.

   1. Where are the (box) _____ of pencils?
   2. The (child) _____ are looking for them.
   3. The (pencil) _____ are missing.
   4. The (bag) _____ of apples is on the counter.
   5. The (distance) _____ around a circle is the circumference.
   6. The (person) _____ at the beach are enjoying the concert.

Circle the correct verb in each sentence.

   7. Jessica (sit/sits) with me every day at lunch.
   8. Devan, Tori, and I (is/are) going to the park.
   9. Esau (ask/asks) for directions to the library.
   10. Jay's collection of rocks (is/are) on display.
   11. The twins' mother (help/helps) them with their homework.
   12. How many eggs (is/are) in a dozen?

Personal Pronouns

Name _____ Date _____

She = Sue

Personal pronouns take the place of nouns.
   Example: Sue gave Todd the book.
                  She gave *him* the book.

Personal Pronouns are *I, me, you, she, her, he, him, it, we, us, they,* and *them.*

Some personal pronouns can be combined with *-self* or *-selves* to form new pronouns.
   Examples: herself   themselves

Write personal pronouns to complete the sentences.

1. _____ gave Marnie directions to the mall.
2. _____ are planning to stay in Florida for three weeks.
3. Troy gave _____ the map.
4. The mayor presented the award to _____.
5. Although _____ won the award, _____ had really done all the work.
6. _____ presented the award to _____ on Saturday.
7. _____ were there when _____ gave _____ to _____.
8. _____ lost his wallet at the mall.
9. Will _____ help _____ find _____?
10. Our teacher said _____ needed to study harder.
11. _____ did it _____selves.
12. When Brett realized what _____ had done, _____ congratulated _____.
13. Would _____ open the door, please?
14. _____ and _____ will arrive at 10:00.

Possessive Pronouns

Yours and Mine

Possessive pronouns show ownership. A possessive pronoun can be used with the name of what is owned or by itself.

Examples: This is *my* watch. The watch is *mine*.
This is *your* chair. The chair is *yours*.
This is *our* home. This home is *ours*.

Possessive pronouns do not have apostrophes.

The possessive pronouns are *my, mine, your, yours, our, ours, his, her, hers, its, their,* and *theirs*.

Write the correct possessive pronoun to complete each sentence.

1. I entered _____ painting in the art contest.
1a. That landscape is _____.
2. Rachel entered _____ watercolor of lilies.
2a. Do you see the one that is _____?
3. Toby didn't finish _____ sculpture in time.
3a. He left the sculpture at _____ house.
4. Did you enter _____ sketches?
4a. Those look like _____.
5. One vase cracked when it fell off _____ stand.
6. Sara and Veronica entered _____ photographs together.
6a. The three with the silver frames are _____.
7. Marc and I worked together on _____ art project.
7a. That mobile is _____.
8. When will the judges make _____ decisions?
9. I was glad _____ family could attend the art show.
10. Sara and Marc said _____ families never missed an art show.

34

© McGraw-Hill Children's Publishing

0-7424-1806-5 *Building Grammar & Writing Skills*

Agreement of Nouns and Pronouns

Name _____ Date _____

She = Aunt, Lawyer, Mother

A pronoun is often used in place of a noun to avoid repeating the noun again in the same sentence or paragraph. Pronouns must agree in gender and number with the nouns they replace.

Singular pronouns take the place of singular nouns. Plural pronouns replace plural nouns.

List four nouns that each pronoun could replace in a sentence. The first one has been done as an example.

1. she	aunt	lawyer	mother	Sally
2. he	_____	_____	_____	_____
3. it	_____	_____	_____	_____
4. they	_____	_____	_____	_____

Underline the pronouns in each sentence. Circle the nouns they replace.

5. Sheila gave her book to Dick.
6. Tom said he would go to the store.
7. The trees dropped most of their leaves last week.
8. Tina and Maria said they would arrive soon.
9. Tori borrowed her brother's bicycle. She put his bicycle away when she finished.

Write a pronoun in each blank. Circle the noun it replaces.

10. The students held _____ pizza party on Tuesday.

11. Our apple tree looks dead when _____ leaves are gone.

12. The cat licked _____ paws.

13. My grandfather lost _____ glasses in the garden.

14. Our team hopes _____ win the game.

Indefinite Pronouns

Name _____ Date _____

Anybody Home?

Most indefinite pronouns end with -*body*, -*one*, or -*thing*. These indefinite pronouns are always singular.

Examples: *Someone* left her purse on the bus.
Is *anyone* missing her purse?

Match a word in Column A with a word from Column B to write 12 indefinite pronouns.

Column A	Column B
any	thing
every	one
no	body
some	

1. _____   7. _____
2. _____   8. _____
3. _____   9. _____
4. _____   10. _____
5. _____   11. _____
6. _____   12. _____

Rewrite the sentences so the pronouns and nouns agree. Remember, the above indefinite pronouns are always singular. The first one is done as an example.

13. Everyone brought their report.
    Everyone brought his or her report.
14. Has anyone done their homework?

_____

_____

15. Somebody found a fossil in their yard.

_____

_____

16. Everyone said the trip to the candle factory was their favorite field trip.

_____

_____

_____

Adjectives

Name _____ Date _____

A Big, Red, Juicy Apple

Adjectives are words that describe nouns or pronouns. *Beautiful, silly, handy,* and *silky* are adjectives.

Adjectives answer these questions: What kind? Which one? How many? How much?

The most commonly used adjectives—*a, an,* and *the*—are also called articles. *An* is usually used before words that begin with a vowel sound.

Underline all adjectives in the sentences, including the articles. Draw an arrow to show the nouns they describe. Some sentences have more than one set of adjectives and nouns.

1. The lonely bird perched on the leafless tree.
2. Our bountiful garden yielded green beans, yellow squash, and ripe tomatoes.
3. I live in the white house with green shutters.
4. The yellow bus stopped at the stop sign at the busy corner.
5. Twenty-five young children rode the school bus this morning.
6. The bus was full of chattering children.
7. A bus driver, careful and patient, drove the rambunctious children to their school.
8. During a January snow storm, school was canceled for three days.
9. Several teachers rode motorcycles to school on warm days.
10. Write five adjectives to describe a person. _____
11. Write five adjectives to describe a lake. _____
12. Write five adjectives to describe an elephant. _____
13. Write five adjectives to describe a chair. _____

(Speech bubbles: "Is that an onion?" "It's a fresh, white onion.")

Name _____ Date _____

Positive, Comparative, and Superlative Adjectives

There are three degrees of adjectives: positive, comparative, and superlative.

Examples:

Positive	Comparative	Superlative
warm	warmer	warmest
popular	more popular	most popular
good	better	best

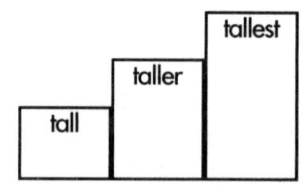

The positive form is used when only one item is being described.
Examples: It is *warm* today.
Football is a *popular* sport.

The comparative form is used to compare two nouns. Add *-er* to the adjective for most one-syllable words and some two-syllable words. For many two-syllable adjectives and all adjectives of three or more syllables, use the word *more* with the adjective to show comparison.
Examples: It is *warmer* today than it was yesterday.
Honolulu is a *more popular* tourist spot than Pittsburgh.

When using adjectives to compare three or more things, add *-est* at the end of the word for most one-syllable words and some two-syllable words. For many two-syllable adjectives and all adjectives of three or more syllables, use the word *most* with the adjective to show comparison.
Examples: Today is the *warmest* day of the year.
Rome is the *most romantic* city in Italy.

Write the comparative or superlative form of the adjective in parentheses to complete the sentences.

1. Of the two roses, the red one is (pretty) _____.
2. Hal is (tall) _____ than Jan.
3. Jan is the (short) _____ girl in the class.
4. *The Hobbit* is the (long) _____ book I've ever read.
5. Who was named the (valuable) _____ player of the Super Bowl?
6. Which of the two doors is (wide) _____?

Hot, Hotter, Hottest

The spelling of some one-syllable adjectives changes when adding -er or -est.

Double the last consonant if the adjective has a short vowel before a final consonant.
Examples: hot   hotter   hottest
big   bigger   biggest

If the adjective ends in -y, change the -y to -i before adding -er or -est.
Examples: happy   happier   happiest
pretty   prettier   prettiest

If the adjective ends in -e, drop the final -e before adding -er or -est.
Examples: paler   paler   palest
white   whiter   whitest

Write the comparative and superlative forms of these adjectives.

	Positive	Comparative	Superlative
1.	practical	_____	_____
2.	simple	_____	_____
3.	silly	_____	_____
4.	red	_____	_____
5.	kind	_____	_____
6.	sad	_____	_____
7.	slow	_____	_____
8.	delicious	_____	_____
9.	strong	_____	_____
10.	straight	_____	_____
11.	humble	_____	_____
12.	clear	_____	_____
13.	loud	_____	_____
14.	clever	_____	_____
15.	big	_____	_____
16.	eager	_____	_____
17.	hard	_____	_____
18.	shiny	_____	_____
19.	difficult	_____	_____
20.	easy	_____	_____

Adverbs

Name _____ Date _____

Now or Later?

Adverbs are words that most often modify verbs. Adverbs answer these questions: When? Where? How?

Examples: We'll go *later*. (When?)
Let's walk *north*. (Where?)
She screamed *loudly*. (How?)

Underline the verb in each sentence. Circle the adverb. Write the question each adverb answers on the line.

1. My grandmother jogs slowly. _____
2. The birds flew south. _____
3. He quickly answered the question. _____
4. We often eat pizza for supper. _____
5. Later, we will visit Uncle Jay. _____
6. She slept peacefully. _____
7. We skated daily last winter. _____
8. Would you like to go shopping tomorrow? _____
9. When he heard the thunder, he looked up. _____
10. She pointed down at the red spot. _____

Write *adjective* or *adverb* on the line to identify the underlined words.

11. _____ The test was <u>easy</u>.
12. _____ She passed the test <u>easily</u>.
13. _____ They followed the <u>north</u> star to freedom.
14. _____ Geese fly <u>north</u> in spring.

Write a sentence with an adverb that answers the question *when*? Circle the adverb.
15. _____
_____

Write a sentence with an adverb that answers the question *where*? Circle the adverb.
16. _____
_____

© McGraw-Hill Children's Publishing 0-7424-1806-5 *Building Grammar & Writing Skills*

Comparing with Adverbs

Name _____ Date _____

Positive, Comparative, and Superlative Adverbs

Like adjectives, adverbs can be positive, comparative, or superlative. Follow the same spelling rules for adding -er and -est.

Examples:

Positive	Comparative	Superlative
early	earlier	earliest
easily	more easily	most easily

Fill in the appropriate form of the adverbs. Use a dictionary if you need help.

	Positive	Comparative	Superlative
1.	_____	_____	hardest
2.	_____	more quickly	_____
3.	_____	_____	most hopefully
4.	patiently	_____	_____
5.	_____	more anxiously	_____
6.	far	_____	_____
7.	_____	more strongly	_____
8.	happily	_____	_____
9.	easily	_____	_____
10.	_____	_____	most cleverly
11.	bravely	_____	_____
12.	_____	_____	nearest
13.	wisely	_____	_____
14.	_____	more gracefully	_____
15.	excitedly	_____	_____
16.	_____	more handsomely	_____
17.	slowly	_____	_____
18.	suddenly	_____	_____

Prepositions

Name _____ Date _____

In, On, Under, and Through

A preposition is a word that comes before a noun or pronoun and shows a relationship to some other word in the sentence.

Common Prepositions

about	above	across	after	along	among
at	before	behind	below	beside	between
by	down	during	for	from	in
into	near	of	off	on	out
over	past	through	to	toward	under
up	upon	with	within		

The object of a preposition is the noun or pronoun that follows a preposition and adds to its meaning.

A prepositional phrase includes the preposition, the object of the preposition, and all modifiers.

Example: Jake and Cassie rode on an airplane.
On is the preposition.
Airplane is the object of the preposition.
The prepositional phrase is *on an airplane*.

Circle the prepositions. Underline the prepositional phrases. Some sentences have more than one prepositional phrase.

1. The roller coaster went up a steep incline and then around a sharp curve.
2. Jon jogged up the street and around the block.
3. The humor in the movie made us all laugh.
4. Kim received a birthday gift from her friend.
5. They sailed across the calm water to the harbor on the other side.
6. After the movie, we went to the ice cream shop for cones.
7. Grandma added seasoning to the turkey.
8. The dog ran under the porch, barked at the skunk, and hid for an hour.

Conjunctions and Interjections

Name _____ Date _____

Aha!

Interjections are words that express strong emotions. When used alone, they are followed by an exclamation mark.

Examples: Help! Ouch! Alas! Oh! Aha!
  Whoa! Wow! Goodness! Oops!

Add an interjection before each sentence.

1. _____ That really hurt!
2. _____ I can't swim!
3. _____ I can't believe you ate the whole thing.
4. _____ What a great job you did on that lawn!
5. _____ That's just what I thought!

Conjunctions are words that join two or more words or groups of words. The most common conjunctions are *and, but, or,* and *nor*.

And connects words or groups of words that are approximately equal.
  Example: Pat *and* Marie washed and waxed the car.

But indicates a contradiction. Use a comma before the word *but* in most cases.
  Example: I like apples, *but* I do not like apple cider.

Or and *nor* indicate a comparison or choice.
  Examples: Would you like to catch the train at 6:00 *or* 7:15?
    Who is better: Troy *or* Brett?
    Neither Mario *nor* Tony came to meet us.

Fill in the appropriate conjunction.

6. William, Edward, _____ Charles were the names of kings.
7. Would you like milk _____ soda with your sandwich?
8. Which do you think is better, the apple _____ the cherry pie?
9. Troy likes cheese pizza, _____ he likes pepperoni pizza better.
10. Spencer likes neither green peppers _____ pineapple on his pizza.

Contractions

Name _____ Date _____

It's About Time

Contractions are words formed by joining two words and omitting some letters. An apostrophe takes the place of the missing letters.

Contractions are often formed by joining a noun or pronoun with a verb.
Examples: we are   we're
I will   I'll
there is   there's

Write the contractions.

1. you are _____
2. he is _____
3. it is _____
4. they were _____
5. you have _____
6. he had _____

Contractions are also formed by joining a verb with the word not.
Examples: were not   weren't
did not   didn't

When *not* is combined with *shall, will,* or *can,* the spelling of the verb changes.
Examples: shall not   shan't
will not   won't
can not   can't

Write the contractions.

7. does not _____
8. was not _____
9. has not _____
10. had not _____
11. have not _____
12. should not _____
13. would not _____
14. could not _____
15. is not _____
16. are not _____
17. will not _____
18. shall not _____
19. can not _____
20. did not _____

Name _____ Date _____

Compound Words

One Plus One = One

A compound word contains two smaller words joined together to make a new word.
Examples: sidewalk　　　toothache　　　lighthouse

Combine words from the list to make 25 or more compound words. Words can be used more than once.

ant	arm	ball	base	basket	bath
bed	berry	bird	birth	black	blue
boat	bow	box	brush	butter	cake
car	chair	corn	cup	day	dog
drop	eater	fall	fire	fish	fly
foot	hair	house	in	light	mail
man	meal	neck	nut	oat	one
out	pan	pea	place	pop	rain
road	room	runner	sand	shine	side
snow	some	star	straw	sun	tail
tea	tie	tooth	tub		

45

Name _____ Date _____

Parts of Speech Review

Fill in the blanks.

1. _____ are words that describe verbs.
2. _____ nouns and pronouns show ownership.
3. Verb _____ is used to express time: to explain what is happening now, what has happened in the past, or what will happen in the future.
4. _____ verbs connect the subject with another word in the sentence.
5. _____ are words that describe nouns.
6. _____ verbs show mental or physical action.
7. Write five prepositions. _____
   _____
8. *Everybody*, *someone*, and *nobody* are examples of _____ pronouns.
9. The _____ form of adjective and adverbs compares three or more items.
10. _____ are words that take the place of nouns.
11. Write two contractions. _____
    _____
12. Write two compound words. _____
    _____

Name the part of speech for the underlined word in each sentence.

13. _____ Paula <u>climbed</u> the tree.
14. _____ A <u>gray</u> squirrel watched her.
15. _____ The squirrel ran <u>down</u> the tree.
16. _____ It threw a hickory <u>nut</u> at Paula.
17. _____ She ducked <u>quickly</u>.
18. _____ Paula continued climbing, <u>but</u> she kept one eye on the squirrel.
19. _____ "<u>Ouch!</u>" she shouted.
20. _____ "Two can play this game," <u>she</u> told the squirrel.

Name _____ Date _____

From Beginning to End

The prewriting stage involves gathering material and ideas. Prewriting activities can include
- Doing research at the library or on the Internet
- Writing an outline
- Taking notes
- Making a time line or flowchart
- Completing a Venn diagram
- Making lists

The drafting stage is the first attempt at writing. The first draft doesn't have to be perfect. You can rework it as many times as needed until you are satisfied. Using a word processor makes it easier to rewrite, change, add, and delete. Some writers prefer to take their time with the drafting stage because it saves time later. Others prefer simply to get their ideas down in a rough form and then go back and spend more time polishing their work.

The revision stage often involves several rewrites. During this part of the writing process, the writer improves the content of the material. You may want to print out a copy of your work at this point and mark changes on the hard copy.

Revising includes
- Polishing
- Adding details
- Expanding on ideas by providing more examples
- Adding vivid descriptive words
- Deleting unrelated material
- Condensing material
- Moving material so it flows better

When you finish revising and making changes, rewrite and print another copy. Now begin proofreading, which involves correcting errors in spelling, grammar, and punctuation. Even if you use a spelling/grammar check program on the computer, you still need to proofread carefully. If you wrote *the* instead of *them*, *he* instead of *her*, or *you* instead of *your*, these errors might not be found by the computer. After you proofread and make corrections, it's a good idea to have someone else read through your work. A second pair of eyes is always helpful.

The final stage in the writing process is publishing your work by either printing it out or handwriting a very neat final copy.

Proofreading

Name _____ Date _____

Proofreading Symbols

Meaning	Symbol
Delete this material	take it out
Insert something here	add word or leter
Replace this letter or word	to be and not to be
Move this word to where the arrow points	Move word to this
Capitalize this letter	jane
Lowercase this letter	Mayor
Remove this letter or word	remove this this word
Close up space	per cent
Change the order of the letters or words	engineer chef
Spell out this word	(1st) (sp)
Add a space	adda space
Begin a new paragraph	¶
Add a period	⊙
Add a comma	∧,
Add a colon	∧:
Add a semicolon	∧;
Add an apostrophe	∨

REMINDER: If you're using a word processing program to write, SAVE your work frequently.

Prewriting: Focus

Name _____ Date _____

Focus on a Topic

Whether you're writing a ten-page report, a one-paragraph essay, or a news article, focusing on a topic is an important prewriting step. If a topic is too broad, it won't be possible to include all the information. If the focus is too narrow, there may not be enough to write about.

Begin to focus on a general topic. The general topic is often assigned by a teacher. Some general topics could include a famous person, birds, your autobiography, the solar system, the history of a sport, or the development of computers.

Once you know the general topic, you'll also need to know the length of the writing assignment. The focus for a one-paragraph descriptive essay would be much narrower than the focus for a ten-page report.

To focus on a general topic, begin by making a list of possibilities. If your assignment is to write a three-page report about a famous person, your list would include famous people who interest you.

1. List six people (past or present) you could write about in a report.

_____ _____ _____
_____ _____ _____

2. List six sports you could write about in a report.

_____ _____ _____
_____ _____ _____

The next step is to narrow the focus even more. If you choose Martin Luther King, Jr., for your report, you would still need to narrow the focus. You could write about his early life, his contributions to the Civil Rights Movement, or his famous "I Have a Dream" speech.

3. Select one person from your list. Narrow the focus to specific areas of that person's life. List three options.

_____ _____ _____

© McGraw-Hill Children's Publishing   0-7424-1806-5 Building Grammar & Writing Skills

Prewriting: Venn Diagram

Name _____ Date _____

Compare and Contrast

A Venn diagram is a useful prewriting tool when doing a comparison/contrast essay.

If your assignment is to write a three-paragraph essay comparing and contrasting two seasons, the first step would be to select the two seasons.

1. Which two seasons would you like to write about?
_____   _____

The next step would be to narrow the focus even more. You could compare and contrast the weather, sports played or another aspect of the two seasons.

2. What would be the focus of your essay?
_____
_____
_____

Fill in the Venn diagram. Use words and phrases related to both seasons in the center where the circles overlap. Write words and phrases unique to each of the seasons in the two parts of the circles that do not overlap.

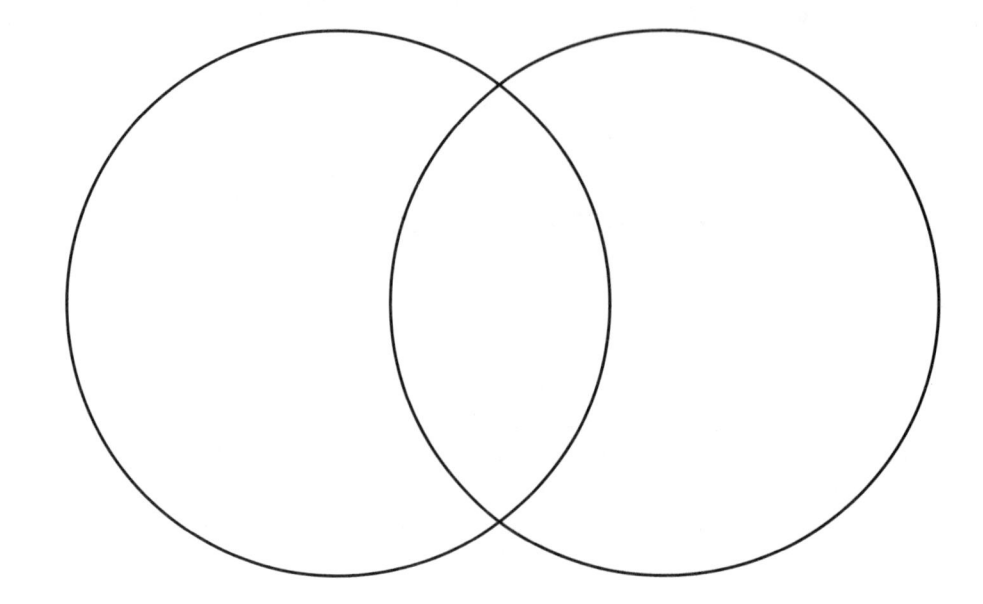

© McGraw-Hill Children's Publishing   0-7424-1806-5 *Building Grammar & Writing Skills*

Prewriting: Outlining

Name _____ Date _____

Preparing an Outline

For many types of writing, preparing an outline is a useful prewriting tool to organize material and ideas.

    This is the format used for an outline.
      I. A Main Idea
         A. An important idea
            1. An example or supporting detail
            2. Another example or detail
         B. Another important idea
      II. Another Main Idea
      III. Another Main Idea

Each main idea in an outline can have two or more other important ideas and examples. In a short essay, each main idea would be a separate paragraph. In a longer report, every important idea and example might be a separate paragraph.

Use the outline format below. On another sheet of paper, complete the outline with information from the last activity (page 50) for a four-paragraph essay comparing and contrasting two seasons. Feel free to add more important ideas and/or examples if needed.

      I. Name of one season
         A. An important idea about this season
            1. A specific example or supporting detail
            2. Another specific example or detail
         B. Another important idea about this season
            1. A specific example or supporting detail
            2. Another specific example or detail
      II. Name of the other season
         A. An important idea about this season
            1. A specific example or supporting detail
            2. Another specific example or detail
         B. Another important idea about this season
            1. A specific example or supporting detail
            2. Another specific example or detail
      III. Ways these two seasons are alike
         A. One way these two seasons are alike
         B. Another way these two seasons are alike
      IV. Ways these two seasons are different
         A. One way these two seasons are different
         B. Another way these two seasons are different

© McGraw-Hill Children's Publishing   0-7424-1806-5 Building Grammar & Writing Skills

Sentence Fragments

Name _____ Date _____

Writing Complete Sentences

Sentences must include a subject and a predicate and express a complete thought.

A simple subject is a noun or pronoun that tells who or what the sentence is about.

A simple predicate is a verb that tells what the subject does, is doing, did, or will do.

In each example, Mary is the subject and the simple predicate is underlined.
    Mary <u>ran</u>.
    Mary <u>runs</u>.
    Mary <u>will run</u>.
    Mary <u>had been running</u>.

A compound subject has two or more nouns or pronouns joined with a conjunction. Compound subjects share the same predicate.

A compound predicate has two or more verbs joined with a conjunction. Compound predicates share the same subject.

A sentence can have a compound subject and a compound predicate.
    Example: Ted, Alice, and Barry hopped, skipped, and jumped.

Incomplete sentences are called fragments.
    Examples: The owl hooted. (complete sentence)
                    Hooted at the moon (fragment: no subject)
                    The owl in the moonlight (fragment: no predicate)

Add a subject or predicate to change the fragments to complete sentences.

1. _____ ran down the hall.
2. Cats and dogs _____.
3. Rain and _____ are types of precipitation.

Underline the subjects. Circle the predicates.

4. Roger and Sara laughed and hugged.
5. Did George arrive?
6. Can Becky Armstrong dance?

Name _____ Date _____

Stop and Take a Breath

A run-on sentence occurs when two or more sentences are joined together without correct punctuation.

> Run-on Sentence Example: Last week I wanted to fly my new kite, but unfortunately it wasn't very windy and began to rain and when I went up on the hill I slid in the mud and twisted my ankle and then the next day when it was good kite-flying weather I couldn't go.

I'm running on and on and on.

Run-on sentences need to be divided into several shorter sentences and rewritten.

> Rewrite Example: I should have known better than to go kite flying on a rainy day without wind. As I climbed the hill, I slipped in the mud. Unfortunately, I twisted my ankle. The next day we had great kite-flying weather, but my ankle hurt too much.

Some run-on sentences simply contain too many unnecessary words. They can be improved by cutting unneeded words.

> Example: I have a brother named Ben and a sister named Meg, and they are my two best friends.
>
> Solution: My brother, Ben, and my sister, Meg, are my two best friends.

Rewrite these run-on sentences on another sheet of paper.

1. Jacob enjoys collecting stamps and coins and he has a baseball card collection too.
2. My three friends all like different sports like Jonah likes football and Marc likes soccer and Sandy likes baseball, but I like swimming more than football or soccer or baseball.
3. Grandpa planted a flower garden with lilies and poppies in the center and he put roses and daffodils around the edges and some marigolds on the right side and daisies on the left and it was a beautiful garden in the summer.

Combining Short Sentences

Name _____ Date _____

He Ran. She Ran.

Although it is important to avoid run-on sentences when writing, too many short sentences sound disjointed.

Two short sentences with different subjects and the same predicate can be joined to make one sentence with a compound subject.

Example: Lisa auditioned for the talent show. Taj auditioned for the talent show.
Combined: Lisa and Taj auditioned for the talent show.

Two short sentences with different predicates and the same subject can also be combined.
Example: Max played baseball on Saturday. Max watched professional baseball on Saturday, too.
Combined: Max played baseball and watched a professional game on Saturday.

If two sentences do not share the same subject or predicate, they can be combined with a comma and a conjunction.
Example: Tristan raked the leaves. His sister put the leaves in a bag.
Combined: Tristan raked the leaves, and his sister put them in a bag.

If two of sentences share the same subject or predicate, combine them as shown in the first two examples. If the sentences have different subjects and predicates, combine them using a comma and a conjunction.

Rewrite these sentences on another sheet of paper.

1. Eric read a book about whales. Aaron read the same book about whales.
2. Aaron learned a lot about whales from the book. Eric learned a lot too.
3. Eric read another book about whales. Eric watched a film about whales.
4. Aaron wrote a report about the book he read. Eric made a poster about the book he read.

54

Topic Sentences

Name _____ Date _____

At the Beginning

A paragraph is a group of sentences related to one topic or idea. The topic sentence introduces the main idea of the paragraph. A good topic sentence is interesting and catches the reader's attention.

Topic sentences can be declarative (A), imperative (B), interrogative (C), or exclamatory (D).
- **A.** Rain forests must be saved or thousands of species of plants and animals will become extinct.
- **B.** Help save the world's rain forests before it is too late.
- **C.** What can be done to save the world's rain forests?
- **D.** "Help us!" shout the plants and animals of the rain forest.

1. Which sentence (A, B, C, or D) do you think would be the best topic sentence for a paragraph about destruction of rain forests? _____ Why? _____
   _____
   _____

Write four possible topic sentences for a paragraph about a funny incident that happened to you.

2. Declaratory sentence: _____
   _____

3. Imperative sentence: _____
   _____

4. Interrogative sentence: _____
   _____

5. Exclamatory sentence: _____
   _____

6. Write a topic sentence for a paragraph about an animal. _____
   _____

7. Write a topic sentence for a paragraph describing a place you have visited.
   _____
   _____

Middle Sentences

Name _____ Date _____

In the Middle

Sentences in the middle of a paragraph can contain examples, descriptions, and details about the topic. All middle sentences should be directly related to the topic sentence.

Write three or more middle sentences for each topic sentence.

1. Wearing a bike helmet could save your life. _____
_____
_____
_____
_____

2. How long can people continue to ignore the poverty in our country? _____
_____
_____
_____
_____

3. Watch out for poison ivy! _____
_____
_____
_____
_____

Name _____ Date _____

Conclusion Sentences

At the End

The conclusion sentence sums up the main idea of a paragraph. It may restate the points made in the paragraph or reach a conclusion based on information or examples given in the paragraph.

These sentences could be conclusion sentences for a paragraph on the dangers of cutting down rain forests.
> Now that you know the facts, are you willing to help?
> Action must be taken now, before it is too late.
> Valuable plants and animals may be lost forever if nothing is done.

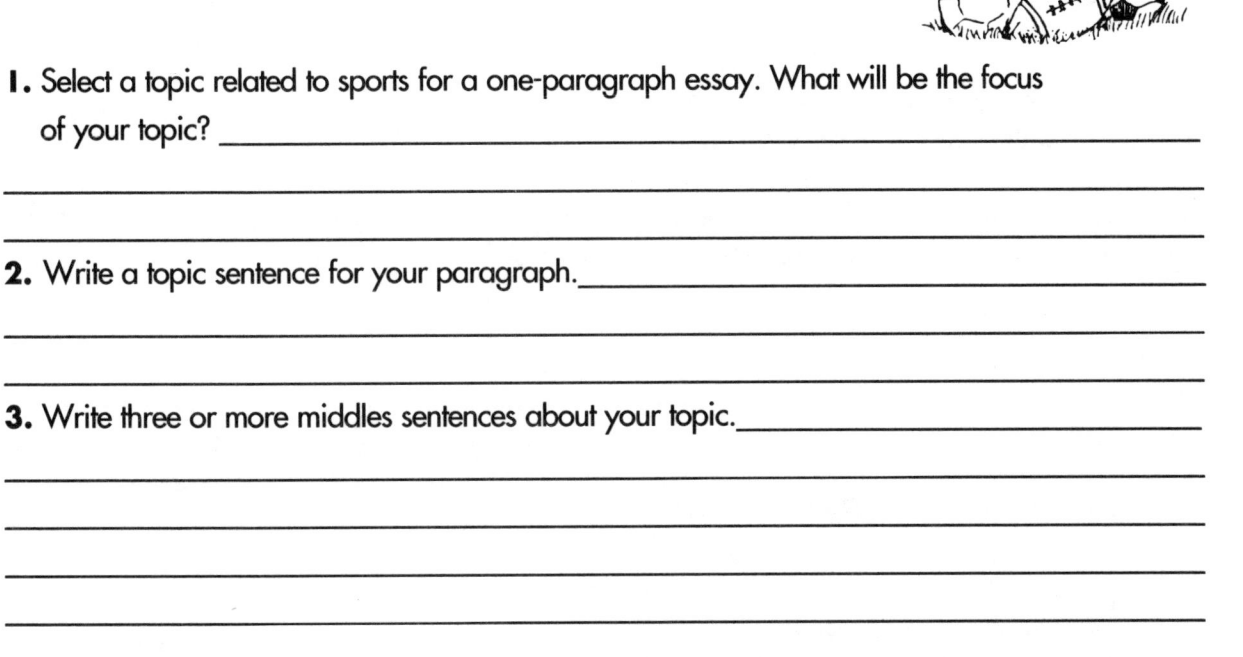

1. Select a topic related to sports for a one-paragraph essay. What will be the focus of your topic? _____
_____
_____

2. Write a topic sentence for your paragraph. _____
_____
_____

3. Write three or more middles sentences about your topic. _____
_____
_____
_____
_____
_____
_____
_____
_____
_____

4. Write a conclusion sentence for your paragraph. _____
_____
_____
_____

5. Go back and reread your sentences. Underline the subjects and circle the predicates in each sentence.

McGraw-Hill Children's Publishing

0-7424-1806-5 *Building Grammar & Writing Skills*

Prewriting: Brainstorming

Name _____ Date _____

Reasonable or Unreasonable?

Brainstorming can be a useful prewriting tool.

Brainstorming can. . .
      produce ideas for writing topics.
      help focus on one aspect of a topic.
      provide ideas for story plots, scenes, and characters.
      provide alternate solutions to specific problems.
      develop a list of pros and cons on an issue.
      allow consideration of various opinions.
      can raise questions to consider.

To complete this group activity, you will participate in a brainstorming session and write a two-paragraph essay about rules of conduct.

1. Before you begin to brainstorm, write two rules of conduct people your age are expected to follow. They can be school rules, family rules, or social rules.

Rule #1 _____
_____
Rule #2 _____
_____

During your brainstorming session, talk about the two rules each member wrote.
      What do members of the group think about each rule?
      Is the rule reasonable?
      Why is that rule imposed?
      Should it be changed?
      What might happen if the rule were changed?

During your brainstorming session, take notes about what people say—even if you don't agree. It's not necessary to write complete sentences when you take notes. Encourage everyone in the group to participate.

2. Use ideas from your brainstorming session to write the first draft of a two-paragraph essay on another sheet of paper. In the first paragraph write about a rule you're expected to follow and why you think it's a reasonable rule. In the second paragraph write about a rule you think is unreasonable and give specific reasons.
3. Revise, proofread, and rewrite.
4. Share your essay with other members of the group.

Name _____ Date _____

Review

Use words from the box to fill in the blanks.

compound	predicate
conclusion sentence	pronoun
focus	run-on sentence
fragment	topic sentence
middle sentences	subject
noun	Venn diagram
outline	verb
paragraph	

1. The _____ in a paragraph provide details and examples about the topic.
2. A _____ is a prewriting tool useful for comparison/contrast writing.
3. The subject of a sentence is always a _____ or _____.
4. The _____ in a paragraph introduces the main idea.
5. An _____ is a useful prewriting tool to organize thoughts and material for an essay or report.
6. A _____ is a group of sentences related to one topic.
7. The predicate of a sentence always contains a _____.
8. The _____ of a paragraph summarizes the main points of the paragraph.
9. To _____ on a topic means to narrow it from broad to specific.
10. Every sentence must have a _____ and a _____ and express a complete thought.
11. A sentence _____ is an incomplete sentence.
12. A sentence with a _____ subject has two or more subjects joined by a conjunction.
13. A _____ occurs when two or more sentences are joined together without correct punctuation. This can also occur when unnecessary words are used in a sentence.

Spatial Order

Name _____ Date _____

Look Up, Down, and All Around

When describing a place, it can be helpful to arrange the information in spatial order, for example, from back to front, top to bottom, or left to right. This technique could be used to describe a small room or a view of the Grand Canyon.

To describe a room, you could begin with an overall impression of the room.

Example: My neighbor's kitchen is so bright and shiny it makes me want to wear my sunglasses.

Each sentence or paragraph could be devoted to one part of the room, like the ceiling, walls, floor, furniture, and decorations.

1. Decide on a room to write about. It could be one at school, at your home, or at someone else's home.

Prewrite. Gather ideas. Write your answers on another sheet of paper.

2. Write one sentence that gives the reader an overall impression of the room and some general information about it.
3. Look up. Describe the color and texture of the ceiling and any light fixtures or fans on the ceiling.
4. Look around. Write words and phrases to describe the color and texture of the walls as well as pictures and other decorations on the walls.
5. Look around. Write words and phrases to describe the furniture, windows, and doors. Include information about the color and texture of furnishings like knickknacks or other items in the room.

Use words like *next to, beside, above,* and *below* to give the readers a sense of where objects are located in relation to each other.

6. Look down. Describe the color and texture of the floor including throw rugs or other items on the floor.
7. Put it all together. Use your notes to write a description of the room.
8. Revise, proofread, and rewrite.

Synonyms

Name _____ Date _____

Laughed, Giggled, Chuckled, and Guffawed

Synonyms are words that mean the same or nearly the same.
   Examples: pretty, lovely, beautiful

A thesaurus is a book that lists word synonyms in alphabetical order.

Writers use synonyms to add variety and make their writing more interesting.

Use a thesaurus. Write five synonyms for each word.

1. saw

2. rich

3. good

4. said

5. ran

6. light

7. picture

Replace the underlined words with synonyms.

8. Freckles is a good _____ dog.
9. I hope you have a nice _____ day.
10. Going to the circus was fun _____.
11. Would you hand me that large box _____?
12. I've never seen a clown with such a sad _____ face!
13. Keagan jumped _____ into the pool.
14. Did you notice Carla's pretty _____ eyes?
15. I couldn't help wonder where you got _____ that great-looking sweater.

Name _____ Date _____

Who Will Read It?

When you write, keep in mind who your audience will be. Your audience is the person or group of people who will read what your wrote.

If you planned to write a story for young children, you would know to use short sentences and simple words.

1. How would a story written to share with your classmates be different from one for very young children? _____
_____
_____

If you wrote a letter to your grandparents, you know they would be interested in hearing about your family, friends, hobbies, how you're doing in school, and other personal information.

2. How would a letter to your best friend be different from one to your grandparents?
_____
_____
_____

If you wrote a review of a new computer adventure game for members of your computer gaming club, you could use jargon and specialized words members would know without needing to explain them.

3. How would a review of the same computer game be different if it were for someone who didn't even know how to use a computer? _____
_____
_____

For each type of writing, describe who the audience might be.

4. An e-mail about a field trip: _____
5. An editorial to a school newspaper: _____
6. A news article about a team's victory: _____
7. An encyclopedia article on Winston Churchill: _____
8. A report on the effects of long-term aspirin use: _____
_____
9. An Internet article on a new rock band: _____
10. A science fiction short story in a magazine: _____

Descriptive Words

Name _____ Date _____

Show, Don't Tell

Writers use interesting words to provide readers with word pictures.

1. Compare these two sentences. Of the two, which paints a more vivid word picture? _____
   A. A girl walked her dog.
   B. A huge St. Bernard pulled a six-year-old freckled girl with pigtails along the path.

Interesting words can be adjectives that describe a person, place, or thing in more detail.

2. For each noun, write three descriptive adjectives that paint a word picture.

car	_____	_____	_____
building	_____	_____	_____
pirate	_____	_____	_____
alien	_____	_____	_____
grandfather	_____	_____	_____

3. How can a thesaurus help you find interesting descriptive adjectives?_____
   _____
   _____

   Caution: Descriptive adjectives help paint word pictures, but if overused, your writing may become too detailed and your reader may lose interest.

As part of the prewriting stage, you can make a list of adjectives related to your topic. When you write, you can add the adjectives throughout the article.

4. Select a topic for a one-paragraph description.
   a flower garden   your pet
   a neighborhood park   yourself
   a brand new vehicle   your bedroom
   a run-down building   a relative

5. On another sheet of paper, list adjectives to describe your topic. Feel free to use a thesaurus.
6. When you finish your draft, revise, proofread, and rewrite.
7. Underline all the adjectives in your paragraph.

63

McGraw-Hill Children's Publishing   0-7424-1806-5 *Building Grammar & Writing Skills*

Lively Verbs and Adverbs

Name _____ Date _____

More Interesting Words

Writers also use lively verbs and adverbs to paint word pictures.
   Examples: The terrified boy darted quickly into the dark alley.
   The elderly couple strolled slowly down the tree-lined avenue.
   A young woman jogged gracefully through the silent park.
   A child toddled unsteadily toward a gaping hole.

Replace each verb with a livelier one. Add an adverb to go with it. Feel free to use a thesaurus.

1. took _____
2. said _____
3. looked _____
4. moved _____
5. laughed _____
6. liked _____
7. reached _____
8. threw _____

Rewrite the following sentences. Use lively verbs, adverbs, and descriptive adjectives.

9. The girl laughed at the cartoon.
_____
_____

10. My mother made a cake that was good.
_____
_____

11. The bus driver drove the children to school in a storm.
_____
_____

12. Preston heard sounds as he walked through the forest at night.
_____
_____

64

© McGraw-Hill Children's Publishing   0-7424-1806-5 Building Grammar & Writing Skills

Author's Purpose

Name _____ Date _____

To Entertain, Inform, and Persuade

Authors write...
       to entertain.
       to inform.
       to persuade.

Determine the author's purpose for each example. Write *entertain*, *inform*, or *persuade*.

1. _____ A newspaper article about a hurricane
2. _____ A magazine article about a new treatment for cancer
3. _____ A humorous article about bathing a dog
4. _____ Directions for building a tree house
5. _____ An editorial about why people should vote in local elections
6. _____ An article about why everyone should take a vacation at the Arctic Circle

Look through newspapers and magazines. Write the title of one article written for each purpose. If possible, cut out the articles and attach them to this page.

7. To entertain:_____
8. To inform:_____
9. To persuade:_____

Circle the purpose that best fits the description.

10. Entertain/inform/persuade: Writing that includes humor
11. Entertain/inform/persuade: Writing that includes personal opinions
12. Entertain/inform/persuade: Writing that includes many facts

Anecdotes

Name _____ Date _____

You'll Never Believe What Happened!

An anecdote is a true account of something amusing or unusual that actually happened. Anecdotes are usually short and do not include much descriptive detail. An anecdote might be about an embarrassing moment, an unexpected surprise, or a time when something turned out totally different from what was expected.

Before you write an anecdote, think about an unusual or amusing personal experience that happened to you or someone you know. It could be something that happened in school or at home. It could be something that happened when you were alone or with others.

1. What will your anecdote be about? _____
_____

The first sentence of the anecdote needs to be interesting. You could begin with a question or an exclamation.

   Example: You won't believe what happened to me on the way home from school yesterday!

2. Write a topic sentence for your anecdote. _____
_____
_____

Since anecdotes are short, every sentence is important. Stick to the topic. Include only relevant details.

3. Write the middle sentences of your anecdote. _____
_____
_____
_____
_____

The punch line is the last sentence of the anecdote. It includes the humor or explanation of why this event was unusual or funny.

4. Write the conclusion. _____
_____
_____
_____

5. Revise, proofread, and rewrite your anecdote. Share it with a classmate, friend, or family member.

Facts and Opinions

Name _____ Date _____

Pizza Tastes Better Than Spinach

Facts are statements that can be proven by checking reliable sources or through personal observation. Opinions are statements of someone's beliefs that cannot be proven.

    Fact: Denver is the capital of Colorado.
    Opinion: Denver is a great place to live.

If many people agree on a statement, that doesn't necessarily make it a fact. "Pizza tastes better than spinach" is an opinion, even if 99% of the people in the world agree.

Write F for fact or O for opinion in front of each statement.

1. ____ Red is prettier than blue.
2. ____ More people buy red cars than blue ones.
3. ____ The climate in Hawaii is pleasant.
4. ____ The climate in Montana is pleasant.
5. ____ The average temperature in Hawaii is warmer than in Montana.
6. ____ Rainy days are depressing.
7. Write an opinion about your city. _____
_____
8. Write a fact about your city. _____
_____
9. When reading or listening to someone speak, why is it important to recognize the difference between facts and opinions? _____
_____
_____
_____
_____

10. Is it appropriate for a reporter to include opinions in a news article? Why or why not?
_____
_____
_____
_____

© McGraw-Hill Children's Publishing   0-7424-1806-5 Building Grammar & Writing Skills

Name _____ Date _____

In My Opinion

An editorial expresses the author's opinion about a topic in a newspaper, magazine, or on a Web site. The purpose of an editorial may be to inform or persuade readers about an issue or situation.

Not every topic you have an opinion about would be a good topic for an editorial. The topic of an editorial is usually something controversial. It could concern a proposed law change or tax increase or be a call for action, such as donating blood or voting for a candidate.

1. Place an X on the lines by the topics that might be used for an editorial.
____ Blue is my favorite color.
____ Our mayor should (should not) be reelected.
____ Too much homework!
____ Why chocolate ice cream is better than vanilla.
____ The need for a neighborhood recycling center.
____ The food in the school cafeteria could be better.
____ Do students need curfews?
____ How much allowance should students receive?

A good editorial clearly explains what the issue is, the author's opinion of the issue, supporting facts, and specific examples to help support that point of view.

2. Write a one-sentence summary of the topic for your editorial. _____
_____
_____

3. State your opinion. _____
_____
_____
_____

4. List supporting facts or specific examples. _____
_____
_____
_____
_____
_____

5. Write the first draft of your editorial on another sheet of paper. Begin it with the *Dear Editor:* salutation.

6. Revise, proofread, and rewrite your editorial. You could send it to your school or local newspaper.

Sequential Order

Name _____ Date _____

Put a Can of Tuna in a Bowl

Some types of writing can best be organized by describing events or steps in sequential order.
Examples: A letter to a friend about events at a party
A description of an exciting baseball game
Instructions for how to build a bookcase
A history report on a Civil War battle

For instruction on how to do something rather simple, each sentence in a paragraph could describe one step of the process. For more complex instructions, you might write one paragraph with details and explanations for each step.

Example of missing details: To make a tuna casserole, first put a can of tuna in a bowl.

Whoops! Does that mean you should take an unopened can of tuna and set it in a bowl? What size bowl? A cereal bowl? A six-quart metal bowl? The directions aren't clear and details are missing. Several steps were skipped and combined into one simple statement.

The directions should have the following: First, open a can of tuna and drain off the moisture. Then, put the tuna in a one-quart bowl.

1. Select one of these topics for a short essay.
   How to kick a field goal
   What I did after school yesterday
   How to mow a lawn
   How to build a snowman
   What I did on my last birthday
   How I learned a great skateboard trick
   How to send an e-mail
   How I chose the name for my pet
2. On another sheet of paper, write steps and put them in order for your topic. Number the steps. Skip several lines between each step.
3. Continue this activity on the next page.

Sequential Order

Name _____ Date _____

Don't Forget the Obvious

1. Read through the steps you wrote. Are any steps missing? Go back and add those steps now. Renumber the steps.
2. After each step, write words and phrases to provide additional details. Include information about tools or materials needed for that step.
3. Don't forget the obvious. If you're explaining how to send an e-mail, don't forget to explain how to turn on the computer and how to open the e-mail program.
Words like *first, second, third, next, then, after that,* and *finally* help clarify the sequence of events.
4. Use your notes to write a short essay on your topic. Continue on another sheet of paper if you need more room. _____

_____
_____
_____
_____
_____
_____
_____
_____
_____

5. Revise, proofread, and rewrite.

Homophones

Name _____ Date _____

Don't Be Confused

When you edit and revise your writing, check for correct spelling and usage of words. Homophones can be tricky because a spelling/grammar check program on the computer will not alert you if you've used the correct word but the wrong spelling.

These are a few homonyms that are often confused.

to	a preposition; towards
too	an adverb; also
two	a noun or adjective; a number
your	a possessive pronoun
you're	a contraction: you are
there	an adverb; in that place
their	a possessive pronoun
they're	a contraction: they are
its	a possessive pronoun
it's	a contraction; it is

Circle the correct words. Use a dictionary if you're not sure.
1. Jon went (to/too/two) the park with (to/too/two) friends.
2. (Your/You're) invited (to/too/two) (there/their/they're) party (to/two/too).
3. (There/Their/They're) hoping you bring (your/you're) swimsuit.
4. (It's/Its) important to use the (write/right) words when you (write/right) an essay.
5. There's (no/know) (way/weigh) Jessie can (way/weigh) more than (one/won) hundred pounds.
6. Ms. Johnson, the (knew/new) school (principal/principle), (made/maid) friends when she gave her speech (to/too/two) the students in the (Jim/gym).
7. (We/Wee) looked forward (to/too/two) the book (sale/sail).
8. (Wood/Would) (ewe/you) (meat/meet) me at the (team/teem) locker room?
9. Walt bought a (pair/pear) of (pairs/pears) for lunch.
10. Why did Tim turn (pale/pail) when he looked in the (pale/pail)?

Name _____   Date _____

Organize by Categories

Peanut Butter and Banana Sandwiches

When writing about a variety of subjects in an essay, material can be organized by categories.

If you were writing about types of foods you like most, you might organize your paragraphs in this way:

> Paragraph 1: My favorite fruits and vegetables
> Paragraph 2: My favorite meats, sandwiches, and main dishes
> Paragraph 3: My favorite desserts
> Paragraph 4: My favorite snacks

You could also organize your material into paragraphs about breakfast, lunch, dinner, and snack foods.

To write a report about games, you could use many different categories. List four games for each category.

Games Using Balls
_____ _____
_____ _____

Games Using Rackets
_____ _____
_____ _____

Games for Two Players
_____ _____
_____ _____

Outside Games
_____ _____
_____ _____

Card Games
_____ _____
_____ _____

Board Games
_____ _____
_____ _____

Team Games
_____ _____
_____ _____

Computer Games
_____ _____
_____ _____

Organize by Categories

Name _____ Date _____

Houseboats, Igloos, and Tents

List four or more possible categories for each of these subjects.

1. Places to live: _____
   _____
2. Clothing: _____
   _____
3. Weather: _____
   _____
4. People: _____
   _____
5. Animals: _____
   _____
6. Chores: _____
   _____

7. Select a topic for a five-paragraph essay organized by categories. You can use one of the above topics or one of your own.
   Topic: _____
   _____
8. Focus of essay: _____
   _____
   _____
9. Three organizational categories you will use: _____
   _____
   _____

10. Follow this format for your essay.
    Paragraph 1: Introduction.
    Paragraphs 2, 3, and 4: One category per paragraph. Include a discussion, description and/or examples of items in each category.
    Paragraph 5: Conclusion or summary.
11. Write your essay on another sheet of paper.
12. Revise, proofread, and rewrite.

© McGraw-Hill Children's Publishing   0-7424-1806-5 Building Grammar & Writing Skills

Name _____ Date _____

Using Reference Sources

For Your Information

Whether you are writing a long report, a short essay, or even a letter to a friend, reference sources can be useful. Reference sources are available in printed and electronic formats.

When checking reference sources, use the most recent material available. Although history itself doesn't change, recent discoveries and newly found evidence or documents may change what people previously accepted as true. New words and terms are added to dictionaries, and the meanings of words can change.

A dictionary lists words and their meanings in alphabetical order. Dictionaries can be specialized, listing only words related to a particular topic, such as medicine, law, or science.

1. Find the name of a specialized dictionary. _____
_____

An encyclopedia contains alphabetized articles that provide information about many topics. Some encyclopedias may be very specialized, containing only articles in one particular field.

2. Write the name of a hardcover encyclopedia available in your library and the name of a multimedia encyclopedia available on CD or online. _____
_____

An almanac contains statistics and lists and is usually published yearly. Although almanacs do not provide in-depth information about a topic, they are useful for finding current information and quick facts.

3. Use an almanac. Find the mailing address of your favorite sports team. _____
_____
_____

An atlas is a collection of maps and other geographic information, such as landforms, political boundaries, capitals, and major cities.

4. Why would it be important to use a current atlas to find the name, capital, and borders of particular country?
_____
_____

74

© McGraw-Hill Children's Publishing　　　　　　　　　　　　　　0-7424-1806-5 *Building Grammar & Writing Skills*

Using Reference Sources

Name _____ Date _____

Where Would You Find It?

For each statement, list one or more reference sources you could use to find the information.

1. You are writing an e-mail to a friend and can't remember the name of a CD your favorite group did last year. _____
_____

2. You want to write a letter to a business and don't know its address. _____
_____

3. Your family plans to move to a new city. You want to learn more about the history of the city.
_____

4. Your family is going to Boston for a vacation. Your parents like to shop at antique stores and visit historical sites. They've asked you to find information for them. _____
_____

5. You and your friend can't agree on who won the 2000 World Series. How could you find out? _____
_____

Use reference sources. Answer the questions. List the name of the source and/or the Web site address where you found the answer.

6. Who won the 2000 World Series? _____
_____

7. What is a meteostat? _____

8. Who was the 18th president of the United States? _____

9. What is the plural of octopus? _____

10. What was Muhammad Ali's name before he changed it? _____

11. The ancient name of this country was Persia. What is it called now? _____

12. What city was once nicknamed "The Mistake on the Lake?" _____
_____

© McGraw-Hill Children's Publishing — 0-7424-1806-5 *Building Grammar & Writing Skills*

Compare and Contrast

Name _____ Date _____

Alike and Different

To compare means to look at ways two or more people, items, ideas, actions, or situations are similar. *To contrast* is to look at differences.

1. Select one of these topics to compare and contrast:

   Goldfish and dogs as pets
   Baseball and football
   Bicycles and motorcycles
   Yourself and another family member
   5th grade to 6th grade
   Watching a movie to reading a book
   Your city to another city
   Living in an apartment to living in a house

2. Use a Venn diagram or other organizational tool to prewrite ideas about both items.
3. Write a short introductory paragraph about the two objects.
_____
_____
_____
_____

4. Write one paragraph that explains how the two are alike. Include examples and descriptive details. _____
_____
_____
_____

5. Write one paragraph describing how the two are different. Include examples and descriptive details. _____
_____
_____
_____

6. Write a summary paragraph that draws a conclusion._____
_____
_____
_____

7. Revise, proofread, and rewrite.

© McGraw-Hill Children's Publishing   0-7424-1806-5 *Building Grammar & Writing Skil*

Advantages and Disadvantages

Name _____ Date _____

Blue or Green?

Part of considering the advantages and disadvantages of two ideas, actions, or other choices is to do a comparison and contrast between the two. Looking at advantages and disadvantages enables you to evaluate your choices and make better decisions.

Select one of these topics to write about.

What would be the advantages and disadvantages of attending school fewer hours each day, but six days a week instead of five?

If you were invited to two events, which should you attend, a party at your best friend's house that might be boring or a different one that might be more fun?

You have a budget for school clothes. Should you buy less clothing that is more expensive and better quality or items that cost less to have more variety?

What are the advantages and disadvantages of eating lunch in the school cafeteria?

What are the advantages and disadvantages of eating out compared to eating at home if both parents work?

1. Write a very brief outline that states the main ideas you plan to write about.

   I. _____
   II. _____
   III. _____
   IV. _____
   V. _____

2. On a separate sheet of paper, begin your essay with an interesting topic sentence and introductory paragraph that grabs the readers' attention.
3. Write paragraphs about the advantages and disadvantages of each option. Include examples and/or specific reasons.
4. Write a conclusion that sums up your essay, clearly states what decision you have made, and why.
5. Revise, proofread, and rewrite.

Cause and Effect

Name _____ Date _____

Because She Was Late

A *cause* is something that makes something else happen. An *effect* is what happens as a result.
    Example: Aunt Jayne was late. (cause)
                       She missed the plane. (effect)

Underline the cause and circle the effect in each sentence.

1. When Aunt Jayne missed the plane, she had to cancel her vacation.
2. Aunt Jayne lost the deposit she had paid in advance when she canceled her vacation.
3. Since she didn't go on vacation, Aunt Jayne decided to spend a week painting the house.

Write a possible effect to complete each sentence.

4. After two days of heavy rain, _____
_____
_____

5. Paul was able to _____
_____
once he learned how to use his new computer.

Write a possible cause to complete each sentence.

6. Todd and Myrna raked for six hours _____
_____
_____

7. _____
_____
_____
Mitchell couldn't find his car keys.

A cause can have more than one effect.
    Example: A snowstorm could cause accidents, transportation problems, and power outages.

An effect can be the result of more than one cause.
    Example: The problems after a snowstorm might be caused by the storm itself, a lack of snow removal equipment, high winds, and very cold weather.

Order of Importance

Name _____ Date _____

The Main Facts First

Information in news articles is arranged by order of importance. The most important information appears in the first one or two paragraphs. Further paragraphs provide additional details, explanations, and background information.

1. Why do you think news articles are arranged this way?
_____
_____
_____

2. Cut out an article from the front page of a current newspaper or print one from the Internet. Select an article that interests you and is at least six paragraphs long.

The beginning of the article should include the most important information.

Read the first two paragraphs. Write short answers.

3. What happened? _____
4. Who was involved? _____
5. When did it happen? _____
6. Where did it happen? _____
7. Why did it happen? _____
8. How did it happen? _____
9. Write a one-sentence summary for each of the next four paragraphs in the article.
_____
_____
_____
_____

10. Read the last paragraph of the article. Compare what you learned in the first paragraph to the information contained in the last paragraph.
_____
_____
_____
_____

Matching

Match the words in the first column with the definitions in the second column.

1. ____ dictionary
2. ____ step-by-step
3. ____ contrast
4. ____ encyclopedia
5. ____ audience
6. ____ order of importance
7. ____ almanac
8. ____ spatial order
9. ____ effect
10. ____ atlas
11. ____ synonyms
12. ____ homophones
13. ____ compare
14. ____ cause

A. The person or group of people who will read what you wrote
B. Words that mean the same or nearly the same
C. Back to front, top to bottom, or left to right
D. The result of a cause
E. A collection of maps and other geographic information
F. A source for statistics and lists published annually
G. Words that sound the same but are spelled differently
H. Sequential order
I. Something that produces an effect
J. Arrangement of facts with the most important first
K. A source that provides definitions of words
L. To look at ways items are different
M. To look at ways items are alike
N. Informative short articles arranged in alphabetically

Writing Ideas

Name _____ Date _____

What If Questions

Asking and answering *what if* questions provides many writing ideas.

A question like "What if Cinderella hadn't lost her glass slipper?" could provide ideas for writing different endings to that fairy tale.

"What if aliens from another galaxy visited Earth?" could provide ideas for science fiction stories.

For each topic, write a *what if* question.

1. computers
What if _____
_____

2. Snow White
What if_____
_____

3. oceans
What if_____
_____

4. dinosaurs
What if_____
_____

5. friends
What if_____
_____

6. feet
What if_____
_____

7. snow
What if_____
_____

8. the president of the United States
What if_____
_____

Save your questions to use with the next activity.

© McGraw-Hill Children's Publishing   0-7424-1806-5 *Building Grammar & Writing Skills*

Name _____ Date _____

What If Answers

A *what if* question can have many different answers.
    Example: What if Cinderella hadn't lost her glass slipper?
    Possible answers: The prince might never have found her.
Cinderella might have married a shoemaker.
The prince might have remained a bachelor.

1. Write two possible answers for this question: What if aliens from another planet visited Earth?
_____
_____
_____
_____
_____
_____

2. Write one of your *what if* questions from the last activity (page 81). _____
_____

3. Write two possible answers to your question. _____
_____
_____
_____
_____
_____
_____

Use any other *what if* question to write a one-paragraph answer.

4. Write the *what if* question. _____
_____

5. Write the answer. Include a topic sentence, middle sentences, and conclusion sentence. Continue on another sheet of paper if you need more room. _____
_____
_____
_____
_____
_____

Narrative Writing

Name _____ Date _____

And Then What Happened?

Narratives describe events or experiences. Events are usually written in the order in which they occurred (chronological order).

Narratives can be factual, such as autobiographies, news articles, and television documentaries or fictional, like fairy tales, short stories, novels, and movies.

Follow these steps for writing a narrative about an experience you've had recently.

1. List ideas for a narrative paragraph. _____
_____
_____
_____
_____
_____

2. Select one idea from your list: _____

3. Narrow your focus. List ideas that narrow the focus of your topic. _____
_____
_____
_____

4. What part of the experience will you focus on in your narrative? _____
_____
_____

5. List words and phrases to describe events related to that specific experience. ____
_____
_____
_____
_____
_____
_____

6. Number the events you listed, in order.
7. Write an interesting topic sentence for your narrative on another sheet of paper.
8. Add middle sentences. Include details and specific information.
9. Add a conclusion sentence to your narrative.
10. Revise, proofread, and rewrite your narrative. Share it with a classmate or family member.

Autobiography

Name _____ Date _____

The Very First Time

An autobiography is an account someone writes about his or her life. An autobiography can cover the most important events in a person's life or one specific event.

Important "firsts" in your life are great topics for an autobiographical essay. Do you remember the first time you lost a baby tooth, walked to school alone, went to a movie, or learned to ride your bike?

1. List other "firsts" in your life that could be topics for an autobiographical narrative. _____

_____
_____
_____
_____
_____
_____
_____
_____
_____
_____

2. Write about a "first" in your life. _____

_____
_____
_____
_____
_____
_____
_____
_____
_____
_____

3. Revise, proofread, and rewrite your narrative. Include a title and photograph if possible.

Interviewing

Name _____ Date _____

Ask Questions

A biography is an account someone writes about another person's life. A biography can cover the most important events in a person's life or one specific event.

You can learn about a person's life by reading books and articles that have already been published. You can also learn about a person by asking him or her questions.

Ask someone you know if you could write a biography about him or her. If you know the person well (a parent, grandparent, or neighbor), you may already know much about the person and even have a specific idea about what aspect of his or her life you might want to focus on for your narrative.

If you don't know the person well, you may need to ask some questions to help you focus on a specific event or time period.

Write ten questions you could ask this person in an interview.

1. _____
2. _____
3. _____
4. _____
5. _____
6. _____
7. _____
8. _____
9. _____
10. _____

Biography

Name _____ Date _____

Gather Answers

Set aside a time to interview your chosen biography. Have your questions prepared. Take along a pencil and paper to take notes. If possible, tape your interview.

Some answers may lead to more questions. That's okay. You can ask questions that aren't on your list. Those are simply to get you started. As you talk with this person, think about a focus for the biography you will write.

Be sure to thank the person for answering your questions.

Complete the rest of this activity as soon as possible after the interview while the information is still fresh in your mind.

1. What is the most interesting fact you learned during the interview?_____
_____
_____

2. What will be the focus for the biography you'll write?_____
_____
_____
_____
_____

3. What would be a good title for the biography?_____
_____

4. List three main ideas you plan to include in the biography._____
_____
_____
_____
_____

5. Write your first draft on another sheet of paper.
6. If you have more questions or need more information, contact the person for a second interview.
7. Revise, proofread, and rewrite your biography. Include a photograph of the person if possible.
8. Give the person you interviewed a copy of the biography you wrote.

Sensory Words

Name _____ Date _____

Sweet, Sour, Bright, Slippery, Loud

We use sensory words to describe the sights, sounds, smells, tastes, and feel of the world around us.

1. Add three more words to the examples for each sense:

Sense	Examples
Sight	round, blue, tiny
Sound	whistle, crack, ka-boom
Smell	burnt, vanilla, musty
Taste	sour, lemony, sweet
Touch	slippery, soft, fuzzy

2. Write sensory words to describe a visit to a deli on a busy morning.

Sights _____

Sounds _____

Smells _____

Tastes _____

Touch _____

Descriptive Writing

Name _____ Date _____

Water, Water All Around

Descriptive writing provides vivid details of people, places, things, and ideas. The key to writing a good description is to be as specific as possible. Using sensory words helps readers see, hear, feel, taste, and smell what you're describing. Authors use many adjectives when writing descriptions.

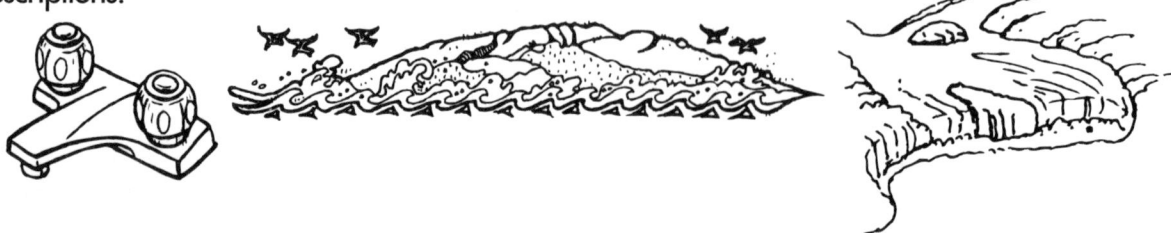

Take something as simple as water and think about ways to describe it. Write your responses to 1–5 on a separate sheet of paper.

Sight: Clear water is different from cloudy water. Water can be dirty, sudsy, blue, or green. Each adjective gives us a different picture of the water.

1. Write more words and phrases to describe the sight of water.

Sound: The sound of a waterfall is much different from the sound of gentle waves on a sandy beach or crashing waves on a rocky shore. As rain, water sounds different, depending on how hard it rains. Ice melting, a dripping faucet, and pouring water from a pail all have different sounds.

2. Write more words and phrases to describe the sound of water.

Touch: Water can be boiling, steaming, luke warm, cool, or icy cold. It can feel gritty, soapy, or clean.

3. Write more words and phrases to describe the feel of water.

Smell: Think about how a clear swimming pool with lots of chlorine smells compared to water in a stagnant pond.

4. Write more words and phrases to describe the smell of water.

Taste: The amount and types of chemicals in water give it many different tastes from metallic to sour.

5. Write more words and phrases to describe the taste of water.

Sensory Writing

Name _____ Date _____

Describe Your Neighborhood

Prewrite: Use sensory words to describe your neighborhood early in the morning in spring and at noon on a very hot summer day.

	Early Spring Morning	Hot Summer Day At Noon
Sights		
Sounds		
Smells		
Taste		
Touch		

On another sheet of paper, write a descriptive narrative about your neighborhood at a specific time of day or season of the year. Include the sights, sounds, smells, tastes, and feel of the neighborhood so vividly that someone who has never been to your neighborhood would be able to recognize it easily.

Elements of Fiction

Name _____ Date _____

Characters, Settings, and Plots

There are many types of fictional stories.
    Examples: mystery, suspense, drama, fables, adventures, tall tales, fairy tales, and science fiction

Long or short, realistic or fantasy, fictional stories have several elements in common: They have characters, plots, themes, mood, settings, and point of view.

All stories contain one or more main characters. Characters can be people, animals, or objects.

1. Who are the main characters in your favorite novel or story?
_____
_____

The setting describes when and where the story takes place. In short stories, the entire story usually takes place in the same place and covers a brief period of time.

Books and movies can include several different settings. The events may take place over several days, weeks, months, or years.

2. What is the main setting for your favorite novel or story?
Place:_____
Time:_____

The plot of a story relates the events that occur. The plot includes what happens to the main characters and how they react.

3. Summarize the plot of your favorite novel or story in one or two sentences.
_____
_____
_____

4. Why do you think events in most stories are arranged in chronological order?
_____
_____
_____

Elements of Fiction

Name _____ Date _____

Conclusions and Themes

In most stories, the main characters face some type of problem or conflict.

1. What type of problem or conflict occurred in your favorite novel or story?
_____
_____

The main characters in a story try to solve or overcome the problem. Sometimes they are successful. Sometimes they fail to solve the problem. Not all stories end with "... and they lived happily ever after."

2. How did the main characters in your favorite novel or story solve or overcome the problem? If they did not solve the problem, what happened as a result?
_____
_____
_____
_____

The conclusion of a story explains how the problem is solved or what happens as a result of not solving the problem.

3. What happens at the conclusion of your favorite novel or story?
_____
_____
_____

The theme is the central idea of a story. Theme is not the same as plot. The theme conveys a view about people and the world. Sometimes the theme is also called the author's message.

The theme may be very positive: If people work together, they can overcome many obstacles.

The theme could be very negative: No matter how hard you try, you cannot beat the system.

4. What is the theme of your favorite novel or story? _____
_____
_____

Point of View

Name _____ Date _____

Someone Has Been Eating My Porridge

Stories can be written from different points of view.

A first-person story is written from the point of view of one character. Only the thoughts, feelings, and experiences of that one character can be included in the story. Events that happen to others can only be included if seen by the character telling the story. What others think or how they feel can be related through dialogue with the main character.

A third-person story is told from the point of view of a narrator who knows what all of the characters are thinking, feeling, and doing.

The story "Goldilocks and the Three Bears" is told from the third person point of view. If the story were told from the point of view of Goldilocks or one of the three bears, it could be a very different story.

Finish the story "Goldilocks and the Three Bears" from the point of view of Baby Bear.

Our porridge was too hot, so Mama, Papa, and I decided to go for a short walk before breakfast. We gathered some nuts and berries and then headed home. I was really hungry by then.

When Papa opened the kitchen door, I noticed right away that something was wrong.

Papa Bear looked at his bowl of porridge. "Someone has been eating my porridge!" he shouted in his deep Papa voice.

I was scared. Who could have been here while we were gone? Was someone hiding in our house?

Mama looked at her bowl. She sounded very worried when she told Papa Bear that someone had been eating her porridge too. Then I looked at my bowl and it was empty! All my delicious porridge was gone. And that wasn't the worst of it.

Continue writing on another sheet of paper. Share your version of the story with a classmate.

92

Name _____ Date _____

Review a Book

A book review includes facts and opinions. Use the elements of fiction to prewrite ideas for a book review. When you finish, write a short review.

Book title: _____

Author: _____

Description of one main character: _____
_____

Description of second main character: _____
_____

Where and when does the action take place? _____
_____

What is the theme of the book? _____
_____

From whose point of view is the story written? _____

Summarize the plot. _____
_____
_____
_____
_____
_____
_____

What is the main problem or conflict the main character faces? _____
_____
_____
_____

How is the problem overcome? _____
_____
_____

How does the story end? _____
_____

Would you recommend this book to others? Why or why not?
_____
_____

Developing Characters

Name _____ Date _____

Bring Characters to Life

Characters can be based on someone you know or read about or can be completely fictional. Any information about the character that is important to the story or that helps the reader understand the character better should be included.

The main character of a story should be someone the reader can identify or sympathize with. Portray characters so that readers care what happens to them.

Even if you don't plan to use all the information in your story, doing a complete character sketch and physical description helps you visualize your character. The better you know your characters before you begin, the easier it will be for you to write about them.

On this page and the next, you'll develop a character that could be used for a short story. Keep in mind the type of stories you enjoy most and might like to write.

The age of the character gives the reader some idea of how he or she will act and react to situations. A three-year-old would certainly act differently in the same situation from a teenager or an adult.

Begin with basic information about your character.

How old is the character? _____   Male or female? _____

A physical description helps the reader visualize the character. Physical attributes can affect how characters act and react and how others react to them.

Height: _____   Weight: _____

Eye color: _____   Skin color: _____

Hair color and style: _____
_____

Other physical traits: _____
_____

Typical clothing this character wears: _____
_____

Save your ideas about this character to use for a short story.

Developing Characters

Name _____ Date _____

Personality Traits

The occupation of a character may give the readers clues about what to expect. Readers would have different expectations from a character who is a student than from one who was a Supreme Court judge. If it's important to the plot, let your reader know whether the main character is a college professor, cowboy, mechanic, Olympic skater, or retired bank robber.

What is your character's occupation? _____

Consider the personality of the character.

What would readers like best about this character's personality? _____
_____
_____

Why would someone like this character as a friend? _____
_____
_____

What would readers like least about this character's personality? _____
_____

What is this character's favorite hobby? _____

What is this character's worst bad habit? _____
_____

What annoys this character most? _____
_____

What makes this character happy? _____
_____

What is the worst thing that ever happened to this character? _____
_____

What is the best thing that ever happened to this character? _____
_____

Where does this character like to spend time alone? _____
_____

Where does this character like to spend time with friends? _____
_____
_____

Other details about his or her personality: _____
_____

Save your ideas about this character to use for a short story.

© McGraw-Hill Children's Publishing   0-7424-1806-5 *Building Grammar & Writing Skills*

Writing Dialogue

Name _____ Date _____

What Did They Say?

Dialogue is the words spoken by characters in a story. Dialogue should be realistic. What they say and how they say it should match the type of characters portrayed.

A young child doesn't use the same words and phrases as an adult. A grandmother who is upset because someone picked all the buds off her flowers would use different words and phrases from a football coach who is upset with the way his team played.

Use quotation marks, commas, and end punctuation correctly when writing dialogue. Begin a new paragraph each time a character finishes speaking.

"Would you like to go to the library book sale?" Trish asked her brother.
"Will they have any art books for sale?" he asked.
"I'm sure they will. Last year I bought two books about Leonardo da Vinci for only a dollar each," Trish told him.
Todd checked to see how much money he had in his wallet.
"I'm ready," he said as he picked up his car keys and headed out the door.

Write dialogue for each situation.

1. A teenager talking to a friend about going to a movie
"_____
_____
_____," said the teenager.

2. A first grader asking for help from an older brother
"_____
_____
_____?" asked the child.

3. The older brother's reply
He replied,"_____
_____."

4. Two sixth-grade girls talking about going to the mall _____
_____
_____
_____
_____
_____
_____
_____

Setting

Name _____ Date _____

When and Where?

Stories can take place in the past, present, or future. The setting can be anywhere on Earth or on another planet. The setting can be realistic or completely imaginary.

Keep in mind the character you developed earlier (pages 94–95). Answer the questions below to describe the setting for a story about that character. Use descriptive adjectives and sensory words.

When does the story take place? _____

Where does the story take place? Be specific. For example: at the base of a volcano, in dark woods, in a land where dinosaurs exist._____
_____

What season of the year is it? _____
What is the weather like?_____
_____

Describe what the character sees._____
_____
_____
_____

Describe sounds the character hears._____
_____

Describe the smells in the air._____
_____

Describe what the character feels._____
_____

Describe what the character might eat or drink._____
_____

Other details about the setting:_____
_____
_____

Save your ideas about the setting to use for a short story.

Story Plots

Name _____ Date _____

Overcoming Obstacles

The plot of a story includes what the characters do, the problems or conflicts they face, the obstacles they overcome, and the consequences of their actions.

In a detective story, the character may face a mental challenge as he or she tries to find clues and solve the crime.

In an adventure story, the character could be faced with a physical challenge, like climbing a mountain or surviving on a deserted island.

A plot could involve personal problems with friends, family, money, or oneself, such as being very shy, getting along with a brother, or making friends at a new school.

1. List two personal problems your character might have to overcome.
_____
_____
_____
_____

A plot could be about the character's need to overcome physical obstacles, like surviving a terrible storm in a small boat, recuperating after a car accident, or being lost in a rain forest.

2. List two types of physical obstacles your character might have to overcome.
_____
_____
_____
_____

Some plots concern tasks that the main character must accomplish in order to win a prize or reward, like killing the dragon to marry the princess. There could also be a penalty for not being successful.

3. List two tasks your character might have to perform and the prize or reward for completing the task successfully.
_____
_____
_____
_____

Save your ideas about plots to use when you write your story.

© McGraw-Hill Children's Publishing   0-7424-1806-5 *Building Grammar & Writing Skills*

Story Plots

Name _____ Date _____

The Quest

Many stories involve some type of quest. The plot could include the character's quest for a specific object (a magic lamp) or a search for the answer to a question (Why did my father leave us?).

1. List two objects your character could be trying to find. Explain why finding the object is important.
   Object 1: _____
   Reason why finding it is important: _____
   _____
   _____

   Object 2: _____
   Reason why finding it is important: _____
   _____
   _____

2. List two questions your character could be trying to answer. Explain why finding the answer is important.
   Question 1: _____
   Reason why finding the answer is important: _____
   _____
   _____

   Question 2: _____
   Reason why finding the answer is important: _____
   _____
   _____

3. Of all the plot ideas you wrote, which one do you like best?
   _____
   _____
   _____
   _____
   _____

Save your ideas about plots to use when you write your story.

Conclusions

Name _____ Date _____

Did They Live Happily Ever After?

In the conclusion of a story, the reader learns how the character completed the quest, overcame the obstacle, solved the problem, or found the answer. As a result, the character usually changes in some way. The character might learn about his or her own strengths or weaknesses, become a better person, become more satisfied with life, or become a hero.

Not all stories end happily. Sometimes a character simply learns to live with a problem and make the best of it.

1. Select one of the personal problems you wrote about. Suggest one way your character could solve the problem. _____
_____
_____
_____

2. Suggest what your character might do if the problem wasn't solved. _____
_____
_____
_____

3. Select one of the physical obstacles you wrote about and a way your character might change by overcoming the obstacle.
_____
_____
_____
_____

4. Select one of the objects or answers your character searched for. Explain whether it was found and what could happen as a result of finding or not finding it. _____
_____
_____
_____
_____

Save your ideas about conclusions to use when you write your story.

Story Writing

Name _____ Date _____

Review and Write

1. _____ in a story can be people, animals, or objects.
2. The _____ is where and when a story takes place.
3. The _____ is the action that occurs in a story.
4. The _____ tells what happened at the end of the story.
5. _____-person stories are written from the point of view of a character in the story.
6. _____ is the words spoken by characters in a story.

Review your notes for character, setting, plots, and conclusions (pages 94–95 and 97–100). Use your ideas to write a story. Save ideas you don't use in this story for another story.

Pay particular attention to the first paragraph of your story. An interesting or exciting opening encourages people to continue reading.

Write your first draft on another sheet of paper. Use strong action words and vivid descriptions as you write.

As you revise and rewrite your story, use this checklist:

- ☐ Did you correct all spelling, punctuation, and grammar errors?
- ☐ Are your characters believable?
- ☐ Is the dialogue realistic?
- ☐ Did you provide enough details for the setting?
- ☐ Did you clearly state the problem or challenge?
- ☐ Is the solution reasonable?
- ☐ Are events arranged in logical order?

Type the final draft of your story on a computer if possible. Title your story. Illustrations are optional.

Friendly Letters

Name _____ Date _____

Dear Friend,

A friendly letter can be handwritten, printed on the computer, or sent as an e-mail. People write letters to keep in touch with each other, to ask questions, to say thank you for a gift or favor, to invite someone to visit, and to let others know what is happening in their lives.

1. When was the last time you wrote a friendly letter?_____
_____
2. Who did you write to?_____
3. Why did you write?_____
_____

When sending a letter by snail mail, include your return address: name, street address, city, state, and zip code. The return address isn't necessary when sending an e-mail.

Always include a greeting followed by a comma.
    Example: Dear Grandpa and Grandma,

What you write about goes in the body of the letter.

When you finish writing, include a closing (Your friend, Love, etc.)

Sign your name.

Friendly Letter Format

Your Return Address

Date (optional)

Greeting,

Body of the letter.

Closing,
Signature

1. On another sheet of paper, write a letter to a friend or relative.
2. Revise, proofread, and rewrite your letter before sending it.

Business Letters

Name _____ Date _____

Thank You for the Wonderful Service

People write business letters to request information or to express opinions, complaints, or compliments.

A business letter includes
    A return address: your name, address, city, state, and zip code. Include your e-mail address and/or telephone number if you want a return call or e-mail reply.
    The current date: month, day, and year.
    The inside address: the name of the person you are writing to, that person's business address, city, state, and zip code.
    The greeting, followed by a colon.
    The body of the letter.
    The closing (Yours truly, Sincerely, etc.) followed by a comma.
    Your signature.

Business letters should be addressed to a specific person if possible. If you do not know the person's name, use a job title (Personnel Director or Toy Division Manager) or a department name (Customer Service).

Include details, examples, or reasons for your opinion, complaint, or compliment. If you are writing about a purchase or service, include when and where the purchase or service took place. If you have questions, be very specific about what you want to know.

1. On another sheet of paper, write a letter to a company or business about a product you purchased or service you received. You could write about the great service at a restaurant or store, a product that worked even better than expected, or a person from the company who went out of his or her way to be helpful.

Business Letter Format

Your return address

Today's date

Inside address

Dear _____ :

Body of the letter.

Closing,
Signature

2. Revise, proofread, and rewrite your letter before sending it.

News Articles

Name _____ Date _____

Who? What? When? Where? Why? How?

The purpose of a news article is to inform readers about events.
News articles are usually written from the third-person point of view. An exception might be an eyewitness account of an event.

1. Cut out and read a news article. Is it written in first or third person?
_____

News should be timely and factual. To be interesting to many readers, news articles are often about national or international events. Articles about local events are usually published only in the areas where readers live.

2. Is the article you cut out timely? _____
3. Does the article you cut out contain facts or opinions? _____
_____

News articles are written in an inverted pyramid style: The most important information is placed at the beginning of the article.

The first paragraph of a well-written news article should be interesting and to the point. Its purpose is to give readers enough information about the event so they have the gist of the story yet want to continue reading.

The first paragraph should answer the questions *who, what, when, where, why,* and *how.*

4. Find the answers in the first paragraph of the article you cut out. If the answer is not in the first paragraph, indicate the paragraph number in which the answer was found.

Who is the article about? _____
What happened? _____
_____
When did it happen? _____
Where did it take place? _____
Why did it happen? _____
_____
How did it happen? _____
_____

104

News Articles

Name _____ Date _____

From More Important to Less Important

The body of a news article contains less important information as the article progresses. The paragraphs in the body of the article are arranged in descending order of importance. The last paragraphs of the article contain the least important information or details.

1. Cut out a news article or use the same one from the last activity (page 104). Compare and contrast the first and last paragraphs. How are they different? _____
_____
_____

Most news articles use many action verbs.

2. List the action verbs from the first paragraph of the article you cut out. _____
_____
_____

Most sentences in news articles are short and to the point.

3. Why do you think that is important? _____
_____
_____

Reporters use familiar words when writing news articles—in general, the simpler the better.

4. Circle the word in each pair that would be better for a news article.

    A. fault   deficiency   D. conflagration   fire
    B. transmit   send   E. awarded   conferred
    C. precipitation   rain   F. climbed   ascended

News articles should not contain unnecessary words. Few adjectives are used in news writing.

5. Rewrite this sentence in 15 words or less. Get rid of all unnecessary words.
    The students at Franklin Middle School visited the U.S. Mint as part of a unit on economics and they learned how new coins are designed, how coins are made, what happens to coins that are damaged, and a myriad of other information and they immensely enjoyed the trip except for Jacob who got lost. _____
_____
_____
_____

Name _____ Date _____

Short and to the Point

Headlines summarize the main ideas of news articles using very few words. Most headlines include at least one active verb.

1. Circle the active verbs in each headline.
   A. Archeologist Discovers Unknown Pyramid
   B. Hurricane Flattens Florida
   C. Parrot Saves Family from Fire

The purpose of a headline is to grab the readers' attention so they want to read the rest of the article.

2. Of the questions *who, what, when, where, why,* and *how,* which questions are answered in headline A? _____
_____

3. Which questions are not answered in headline B? _____
_____

4. Of the three headlines (A, B, or C), which do you think is most likely to grab a reader's attention? ____ Why? _____
_____
_____

5. Why do you think newspapers use large size type for headlines? _____
_____

6. Write a headline for each event. Use six words or less and at least one active verb in each headline.
   Something that happened at school yesterday: _____
   _____
   _____

   A recent sports event you watched or participated in: _____
   _____
   _____

   A family holiday: _____
   _____
   _____

   The most memorable day of your life: _____
   _____
   _____

News Writing

Name _____ Date _____

You're in the News

Prewrite ideas for a news article. Answer the questions about an event you saw or attended recently.

1. Who was involved? _____
_____

2. What happened? _____
_____
_____
_____

3. When did it happen? _____
4. Where did it happen? _____
5. Why did it happen? _____
_____
_____
_____

6. How did it happen? _____
_____
_____
_____

7. What happened as a result? _____
_____
_____
_____

8. Write a headline summarizing the main idea of your article. _____
_____

9. Write your news article on another sheet of paper. Include a headline in large print.

   Remember: The first paragraph should contain the most important information and answer *who, what, when, where, why,* and *how.*

Use familiar words, active verbs, and short sentences. Eliminate unnecessary words.

Short Story Writing

Name _____ Date _____

The Fall from the Wall

A nursery rhyme, picture, news article, poem, or cartoon could be a good start for a short story idea.

To write a short story based on the nursery rhyme "Humpty Dumpty," you could start by asking questions.

Write answers to these questions about the poem.

1. Why did Humpty Dumpty sit on the wall? _____
_____

2. What kind of wall was it? _____
3. When and where did this take place? _____
_____

4. What caused him to fall? _____
_____

5. Why were the king's horses and men nearby? _____
_____

6. If they couldn't put Humpty together again, what happened to him? _____
_____

7. Write two additional questions and answers about the nursery rhyme "Humpty Dumpty."
_____
_____
_____
_____

8. Write two questions and answers about any other nursery rhyme or poem.
   Title of nursery rhyme or poem: _____
_____
_____
_____
_____
_____

9. On another sheet of paper, write the first draft for a short story based on any nursery rhyme or poem.
10. Edit, revise, and proofread your story before writing the final draft. Be sure to add a title. Illustrations are optional.

Name _____ Date _____

Book Reports with a Twist

Are you tired of writing the same type of dull, boring book reports you've been doing for years? Try one of these interesting and fun options.

    Draw a four- to six-panel cartoon with speech balloons to show the main events.
    Write a poem about the plot.
    Rewrite the plot as a short play.
    Do a character sketch of the main character.
    Write a dialogue between yourself and the main character discussing events in the book.
    Write a news article about events in the book.
    Create a poster showing important scenes from the book.
    Imagine being a reporter. Interview the main character by writing questions and the character's answers.
    Write an e-mail to the main character and the character's reply.
    Rewrite the plot as a fairy tale or fable.
    Dress up like the main character and give an oral presentation about the character.
    Write a different ending for the story.
    Write a sequel to the story. Explain what happened after the story ended or several years later.

Somewhere in your report you should include the title of the book and the author's name. This information could appear in the right-hand corner or as a heading on the top of the first page.

1. Be creative. Use ideas from the list above or your own ideas. Describe the approach you will use for your book report. _____
_____
_____
_____
_____
_____

2. Write a book report on another sheet of paper.

3. When you finish your book report, revise, proofread, and rewrite.

Reports

Name _____   Date _____

A History of the World from Then Until Now

A report summarizes material available on a given subject. When writing a report, people use information already known to present facts about a topic in an interesting and exciting way.

When report topics are assigned, they are usually quite broad. The first step in writing a report is to choose the topic and focus on one aspect of that topic. The focus should be narrow enough to be manageable, but not so narrow that you can't find enough information to report. If you focus on a topic that interests you, your report will be more fun to write.

If your assignment is to write a report about insects, you can focus on one type of insect or one area of insect behavior that interests you. You could do some research at the library or on the Internet to help you focus on your topic. You could talk to a scientist who studies insects or to a person who raises bees.

1. What else could you do to narrow the topic and find one that interests you? _____
_____
_____
_____

2. What will be the focus for your report? _____
_____

Once you focus on a topic, make a list of questions you could answer in your report. By having specific questions in mind, you can look for specific answers as you do your research. As you learn more about your topic, you will probably think of more questions.

    Topic: Insects
    Focus: Lightning bugs
    Questions: What do they look like?
                        How do they produce light?
                        What do they eat?

3. List three other questions about lightning bugs.
_____
_____
_____

4. On another sheet of paper, list questions for your topic.

References

Name _____ Date _____

Begin Your Research

Once you have a focus and a list of questions, begin your research. It can be helpful to write each question on a separate sheet of paper. As you find answers, make notes on the page with the question. This helps organize material for an outline.

Print or photocopy illustrations, maps, tables, graphs, or other types of material to include in your final report.

The types of reference sources you use will depend on your topic. Dictionaries, encyclopedias, almanacs, atlases, magazines, newspapers, and reference books are available in both print and electronic forms.

A bibliography lists sources used and is included at the end of a report. You will need this information for a bibliography:

    Titles of books or articles (print or electronic)
    Authors of books or articles (print or electronic)
    Volume number of books in a set
    Page numbers of quotations used
    Page numbers of magazine, newspaper, and encyclopedia articles
    Publication date including day, month, and year if listed
    Publishers of books
    City, state, and/or country where sources were published
    Internet addresses of online sources
    Names of people interviewed and dates of interviews

The information in a bibliography must be listed in a specific order and is different for different types of sources. Punctuation is also very specific. You can find sample formats for writing a bibliography at the library and on the Internet.

Use the computer catalog at the library and an Internet search engine to locate material. If needed, ask your teacher, librarian, or parent for help.

On a separate sheet, list three specific library sources and three Internet addresses you could use to find more information about your topic.

Report Writing

Name _____ Date _____

Organize Before You Write

The next step in writing a report is to make an outline (page 51). Use your questions and the notes you wrote while doing your research to create an outline.

Arrange your questions in a sequential or other logical order. Each question could be a main idea for your outline. The answers you found could be the important ideas, examples, and supporting details in your outline.

1. On another sheet of paper, prepare an outline for your report.

Use your outline and notes to write the first draft of your report. Although you don't need to be too concerned with spelling, grammar, and punctuation at this stage, remember that the better your first draft is, the less work you'll need to do later.

Keep these points in mind as you write, revise, and edit your first draft.

> Begin your report with an interesting topic sentence.
> Explain the scope of your report in the first paragraph.
> Use interesting words and sentences.
> Write a separate paragraph for each new main idea.
> Organize your paragraphs in a logical order.
> Write your report in your own words.
> Use transitional sentences to lead from one paragraph to the next.
> Include a conclusion paragraph that summaries the main points of your report.

2. Write the first draft of your report. Use a computer word processing program if possible.
3. Edit, revise, and proofread your first draft.
4. Add copies of illustrations or other types of graphics to enhance your report.
5. After you complete the final rewrite, set your report aside for a day. Go back and read it carefully one more time to see if you need to make any changes or corrections. Add a cover page that includes the title of your report, your name, and the date.

True or False?

Circle *T* for true or *F* for false.

1. T F All well-written stories have a happy ending.
2. T F A bibliography is an account of someone's life.
3. T F When and where a story takes place is part of the setting.
4. T F A narrative describes events or experiences.
5. T F Asking and answering *what if* questions can provide many writing ideas.
6. T F Animals can never be the main characters of stories.
7. T F There is only one possible answer to any *what if* question.
8. T F An interview with the person you are writing about is a good way to begin writing a biography.
9. T F The theme of a story is the same as the plot.
10. T F A third-person story is written from the point of view of three main characters.
11. T F The only reason people write business letters is to complain.
12. T F An autobiography is an account someone writes about another person's life.
13. T F You should use a closing for both a business letter and a friendly letter.
14. T F Fairly tales, fables, and documentaries are examples of narratives.
15. T F Words that describe the sights, sounds, smells, tastes, and feel of objects are called sensory words.
16. T F A narrative is usually not written in chronological order.
17. T F In a news article, the most important information is presented in the final paragraph.
18. T F To focus on a topic means to narrow it down.

Hyperbole

Name _____ Date _____

Leap Tall Buildings

Hyperbole is extreme exaggeration, often used in tall tales—stories about super characters with extraordinary abilities.
    Example: Superman can leap tall buildings in a single bound.

1. List unusual abilities of other super characters you've read about or seen on television or movies.

Character's Name	Ability
_____	_____
_____	_____
_____	_____
_____	_____

Hyperbole can also be a statement that everyone knows is an exaggeration: "I'm so hungry I could eat an elephant."

2. Finish these statements with hyperbole.

Josh could run faster than_____
Mari could see as far as_____
Jeb was stronger than_____
Teri was smarter than_____
Brett could throw a ball _____
Jessica could_____

To write a tall tale, begin by creating a super character. Super characters can be male, female, animal, or even nonliving objects like a supercomputer, crime-fighting frying pan, or magic luggage. Superheroes are bigger, stronger, faster, smarter, etc., than anyone else.

Name of your super character:_____
Unusual abilities:_____
_____
_____
_____

Save your ideas to use with the next activity.

Name _____   Date _____

Tall Tale Plots

Super Character Saves Earth

Tall tales are basically adventures stories. The plot is the most important part of the story. Since most tall tales are short, character development and setting are of lesser importance.

In a tall tale, the super character faces a specific task that must be completed in an unusual or humorous way. The main purpose of a tall tale is to entertain.

Using the super character and abilities you developed in the last activity (page 114), write ideas about what your super character might do in each situation. Use exaggerated details.

1. Your super character is caught alone in a terrible blizzard. How does your super character beat the storm? _____
_____
_____
_____

2. Your super character is lost in a rain forest without any food or water. What happens?
_____
_____
_____
_____

3. Unfriendly aliens have invaded Earth. How will your super character save the world?
_____
_____
_____
_____

4. An evil computer is trying to take over the government. What will your super character do?
_____
_____
_____
_____
_____

Save your ideas to use with the next activity.

Writing Tall Tales

Name _____ Date _____

To the Rescue

A tall tale is like other fiction stories: It has a main character, a setting, a plot, and a conclusion.

1. Read a tall tale at the library or on the Internet. Some tall tale characters are Paul Bunyan, Pecos Bill, Slewfoot Sue, John Henry, Johnny Appleseed, and Tony Beaver.
2. Fill in the blanks to write a tall tale. When you finish, add a title.

_____
(title)

_____ was the _____ person in
(name of super character)   (a superlative adjective)

_____. Everyone knew _____
(name of a place)   (name of super character)

could _____.
(type of super action or ability)

One day _____ met a wicked _____
(name of super character)   (person or thing)

who tried to _____
(an action)

All of his/her friends and neighbors quaked in fear, but not _____.
(name of super character)

As soon as he/she realized what was happening, he/she
_____.
(an exaggerated action)

That was the end of the wicked _____. Everyone
(person or thing)

cheered. And that's how _____ earned the
(name of super character)

nickname _____.
(a nickname for the super character)

2. On another sheet of paper, prewrite a tall tale about your super character.
3. Edit, revise, and proofread your tall tale before writing the final draft. Be sure to add a title. Illustrations are optional.

Writing Poetry

Name _____ Date _____

Poetry

Poetry is the first type of formal language young children usually hear. Before they are ready to understand stories, they enjoy the rhymes and rhythms of Mother Goose and other short poems.

1. What was your favorite rhyme when you were little? _____

2. Why did you like it? _____
_____
_____

Like prose, poetry comes in many forms and styles and has many different purposes. People write poetry to entertain, to tell stories, to paint word pictures, and to express thoughts and feelings. Some poems are very short; some are very long. Some poems rhyme. Some don't.

3. Do you prefer to read poetry or prose? Why? _____
_____
_____

4. Do you prefer to write poetry or prose? Why? _____
_____
_____

5. What is the name of your favorite poem? _____
_____
_____

Read a poem. Then answer the questions.

6. What is the title? _____
7. Who wrote it? _____
8. Why do you think the poet wrote this poem? _____
_____

9. What is the mood of the poem? (How does it make you feel?) _____
_____

10. What is your opinion of the poem? _____
_____
_____

End Rhymes

Name _____ Date _____

The Moon in June

Many poems use a pattern of end rhymes: The last words of lines rhyme in specific patterns.

The example below uses the rhyme pattern common in limericks.

> What Did I See?
> As a drove along, I saw a strange sight
> On my way to a movie last Saturday night.
> Was it a UFO?
> I really don't know.
> But it certainly gave me a fright!

1. Which three lines use the same end rhyme? _____

2. Which two lines rhyme with each other? _____

Rhyming words can be one syllable, like *sight*, *night*, and *fright*.

3. Write four more one-syllable words that rhyme with *night*. _____
_____ _____ _____

Rhyming words can be more than one syllable, as long as the last syllables rhyme. *Stoplight*, *eyesight*, and *headlight* all rhyme with *night*.

4. Write two other words of more than one syllable that rhyme with night.
_____ _____

5. For each word, write ten or more words that rhyme.

forsake: _____
_____
_____

soon: _____
_____
_____

goes: _____
_____
_____

try: _____
_____
_____

Writing Jingles

Name _____ Date _____

Give a Hoot: Don't Pollute

Jingles (also called slogans) are short poems used to relay messages that are easy to remember. Companies use jingles to help sell products.

Example: Try the rest.
Then buy the best.

1. How do you think jingles help sell products? _____
_____
_____

To write a jingle, begin with the first line. Make a list of words that rhyme with the last word of the first line. Use one of the rhyming words to end the second line. You may need to try several different first lines before you find one that works.

2. List words that rhyme with *treat*. _____
_____
_____

3. Finish this jingle. Use any product, real or imaginary.
If you're hungry for a treat, _____
_____

Jingles can be used as slogans for political campaigns.
    Example: Vote for Stan!
                He's the man!

4. Write a rhyming campaign jingle using your name. _____
_____
_____

Jingles can encourage people to act in specific ways.
    Example: Give a hoot,
                Don't pollute.

5. Write a rhyming jingle to encourage people to act in a specific way. Suggestions: wear a bike helmet; get lots of exercise; eat healthy foods; don't use drugs; be kind to others.
_____
_____
_____

Writing Haiku

Name _____ Date _____

Winter

Haiku are very formal non-rhyming poems. The topic of a haiku is usually related to nature or a season. The purpose of a haiku is to paint a vivid word picture or express strong feelings about nature.

Each haiku poem is three lines long. The first and third lines contain five syllables. The second line contains seven syllables.

1. Read the example. Write the number of syllables on the blanks for each line.

                    Winter
         _____ Snow falls silently
         _____ Shrouding Earth in a blanket
         _____ As winter descends.

To write a haiku about a season, select the season.

2. What season would you like to write about? _____

3. Write words and phrases to describe that season. _____
_____
_____

4. Prewrite your poem on scrap paper. Feel free to cross out, rearrange words and phrases, and rewrite as often as needed. Count the number of syllables in each line.

5. When you finish, write your haiku below. Add a title.

            _____
_____
_____
_____

6. Use the same method to prewrite a haiku about something in nature, like an animal, a beautiful tree, weeds, or a peaceful lake.

7. When you finish, write your second haiku here.

            _____
_____
_____
_____

© McGraw-Hill Children's Publishing   0-7424-1806-5 Building Grammar & Writing Skills

Writing Metaphor Poems

Name _____ Date _____

The Cloud Is a Pillow

Metaphors are figures of speech that compare two unlike objects without using the words *like* or *as*.

Examples: Security is a fuzzy blanket.
Contentment is a purring cat.
My sister is a giggle box.
My friend is a pillar of courage.

Metaphors are often used in poetry.

Write an adjective and a noun or a noun phrase (noun plus a prepositional phrase) to complete each metaphor.

1. Love is_____
2. Happiness is_____
3. Freedom is _____
4. Kindness is_____
5. Courage is_____
6. My brother is_____
7. My friend is_____
8. I am_____
9. Prewrite a metaphor poem on scrap paper. Use a metaphor for the first line. Add at least four more lines. Your poem does not need to rhyme, but it can. Example:

Life
Life is a bowl of spaghetti
With lots of loose ends and tangles.
Spices add variety and flavor.
Each bite, a bit different,
Each day, a new adventure.

10. Write the final version of your poem with a title.

_____
_____
_____
_____
_____
_____

Writing Acrostic Poems

Name _____ Date _____

Acrostics

An acrostic poem uses a topic word as the theme of the poem. The topic word could be a person's name (or your own), the name of a place, a season, a month, a holiday, an activity, or an object.

The first word of each line of the poem begins with a letter in the topic word.

To write an acrostic poem about cats, the first word in the first line begins with C. The first word in the second line would begin with A, etc.

An acrostic can be very short.

Example: Cats
Are
Too
Sneaky.

An acrostic poem can be much longer.

Example: Cathy cuddles with her kitten
And feels contentment.
The sound of its purrs provides
Security and comfort.

1. Prewrite an acrostic poem.
   Write your topic word on lined paper, one letter to each line. Skip a few lines between each letter.
   Write words and phrases that begin with the letter for each line. Add other related words and phrases about the topic. Use a thesaurus if you need more word ideas.
   Polish your poem until it is focused on your topic.
   Capitalize the first word of each line and sentence. Check spelling and grammar.

2. Write the final version below.

_____
_____
_____
_____
_____
_____
_____

Writing Repetitive Poems

Name _____ Date _____

Repetition

Some poems like "Mary Had a Little Lamb" and "London Bridge" use repetition of words or phrases. This makes the poems easy to memorize and sing.

Another example is the song/poem, "The Wheels on the Bus."

> The Wheels on the Bus
> The wheels on the bus go
> Round and round,
> Round and round,
> Round and round,
> The wheels on the bus go round and round,
> All through the town.

1. Use repetition to finish these poems.
   For poem 1, use the same style as "The Wheels on the Bus."
   My friend and I shout, "_____"
   "_____"
   _____.
   My friend and I shout, "_____"
   _____.

For poem 2, use the same style as "Mary Had a Little Lamb."

_____ had a _____

_____ , _____

_____ had a _____

_____.

For poem 3, use the same style as "Row, Row, Row Your Boat."

_____
_____
_____
_____

2. Write a second verse for each of your poems on another sheet of paper.

123

Name _____ Date _____

Revising and Editing Checklist

Grammar, Spelling, and Punctuation
___ Do all sentences begin with a capital letter?
___ Do all sentences have end punctuation?
___ Do all sentences have subjects and predicates?
___ Do subjects and predicate agree?
___ Are all words spelled correctly?
___ Are all proper nouns capitalized?
___ Do all sentences make sense?

Paragraph Writing
___ Did you begin with an interesting topic sentence?
___ Does your topic sentence express the main idea?
___ Do the middle sentences stick to the main idea?
___ Did you include specific examples?
___ Are the main points presented in the right order?
___ Is any important information missing?
___ Is there too much information?
___ Does the conclusion sentence sum up the main idea?

Essay Writing
___ Did you focus on a topic?
___ Is the introductory paragraph interesting?
___ Are paragraphs arranged in a logical order?
___ Did you include specific examples?
___ Did you include enough detail?
___ Did you include too much detail?
___ Does the conclusion paragraph summarize your main idea?